THE
REALITY
OF
RETIREMENT

THE
REALITY
OF
RETIREMENT

The Inner Experience of
Becoming a Retired Person

JULES Z. WILLING

William Morrow and Company, Inc.
New York   *1981*

Grateful acknowledgment is made for permission to reprint the following material quoted in *The Reality of Retirement*:

"Bittersweet Farewell of a Grown-up Child" by Randi Kreiss, published March 22, 1979, in *The New York Times*, copyright © 1979 by The New York Times Company. Reprinted by permission.

"Private Lives" by John Leonard, published March 28, 1979, in *The New York Times*, copyright © 1979 by The New York Times Company. Reprinted by permission.

"Facing Up to Retirement: More Companies Help Ease the Way" by Leslie Bennetts, published August 20, 1979, in *The New York Times*, copyright © 1979 by The New York Times Company. Reprinted by permission.

Excerpt from Sydney J. Harris's column of September 8, 1979, from the *Chicago Sun-Times*, copyright © 1979 by Sydney J. Harris. Reprinted by permission of Sydney J. Harris and Field Newspaper Syndicate.

Excerpt from *Earthwalk* by Philip Slater, copyright © 1974 by Philip E. Slater. Reprinted by permission of the author.

Excerpt from "Age Prejudice in America" by Dr. Alex Comfort, published in *Social Policy*, November/December 1976, copyright © 1976 by Alex Comfort. Reprinted by permission of the author.

Excerpt from "Learn to Grow Old" by Dr. Paul Tournier, copyright © 1972 by Paul Tournier. Reprinted by permission of the author.

Library of Congress Cataloging in Publication Data

Willing, Jules Z
    The reality of retirement.

    1. Retirement—Psychological aspects.
I. Title.
HQ1061.W54   305.2'6   80-21919
ISBN 0-688-00298-6
ISBN 0-688-00394-X (pbk.)

Printed in the United States of America

First Edition

1 2 3 4 5 6 7 8 9 10

BOOK DESIGN BY BERNARD SCHLEIFER

To Cory,
*my partner in marriage,
in retirement, and in the making of
this book*

ACKNOWLEDGMENTS

"EVERYTHING IS CONNECTED to everything else." This law of ecology, it seems to me, may also apply to books, for a book is developed in an environment provided largely by the author but importantly sustained by many others.

In addition to my wife, Cory, who contributed beyond all recounting, those who were part of the ecology of this book include my son and daughter, Donald and Susan, who had their separate experiences of my retirement and who have generously permitted me to describe events usually held in family privacy; Melvin J. Fox, who in a way typical of his friendship cleared for me a major obstacle on the road to publication; the remarkable women of The Grail in Cornwall-on-Hudson where this book was begun; Ronah and Harold Posner, whose warm and sustained hospitality contributed so greatly to its completion; Donald D. Greenstein, who helpfully provdied pension expertise for Chapter XXV, and the many men and women who shared their thoughts and feelings with me.

For permission to quote from their work, I am grateful to Dr. Paul Tournier, Alex Comfort, M.D., Warren A. Peterson, Ph.D., Leslie Bennetts, Randi Kreiss, John Leonard, Philip E. Slater, Ph.D., and Sydney J. Harris.

CONTENTS

INTRODUCTION

TOO MUCH ABOUT retirement is unspoken, and each of us who conceals his secret feelings and private fears becomes a participant in what amounts to a conspiracy of silence.

Retirement is by no means ignored; on the contrary, it is widely discussed and written about. What is not said is how it feels: the inner experience of it. It is considered bad form to be anything but cheery and superficial about what is happening when a person retires, so that we all tend to behave with a certain amount of pretense, like visitors in a sickroom. Thus we are prevented, and in turn prevent others, from seeing and acknowledging what really goes on.

The unanswered question is not so much what happens *to* people when they retire as what happens *in* people when they retire. As long as this question remains unanswered or —worse—is answered inaccurately, each of us must experience retirement as though we were the first to enter it. We are surprised by the strength and depth of our own emotions. We have no way of knowing whether others feel as we do or, indeed, of knowing what feelings are appropriate. For many of us, who are not used to being in touch with our own feelings, there is the problem of not knowing what to do about what we feel.

A question that troubles me greatly is—why this secrecy?

To understand this, I think, one must know the answer to the question—what is the secret?

I do not pretend to have a complete or final answer to either question, but I can suggest some answers that seem to ring true. My knowledge of what others feel is necessarily limited to the people who shared their feelings with me, not in formal or structured interviews, but in real-life encounters, spontaneous responses to my own willingness to share with them my feelings about my own retirement.

These people are mostly executives or professionals who have had positions of authority and responsibility in business and at the managerial level in government and education. They are primarily middle-class or upper-middle-class, white, and urban, and they usually have adequate or generous pensions. As is typical of today's pensioners, they are mostly men, although the retired career women I have talked with did not seem to differ greatly from the men in their reactions.

The experience of retirement as I will describe it is probably very different from that of blue-collar workers and rank-and-file civil service employees. It is certainly different from those whose incomes are limited to Social Security or disability pensions.

Because formal retirement today is still primarily a male experience, it is natural that I should write mostly about men, and I am very much aware that what I say is said from my own male perspective; this is unavoidable. But I think it may be useful and instructive for the significant women affected by a man's retirement—wives, daughters, and others—to learn what some men think and feel about aspects of their lives that women very rarely share, and also some aspects of living commonly left primarily to women.

I will not include in my discussion the people who take their pensions and start second careers, because I do not consider them to be retired. I am describing the executive who has come to the end of his career. What happens to him when he leaves the world of work and enters retirement?

More of us do so each year. In the United States in 1900 there were 3 million people who were past sixty-five. In 1975, there were 22 million and by 2025, there will be 45 million. If we consider people between the ages of forty-five and sixty-four to be potential retirees, more than 20 percent of the American people were in the preretirement range in 1970.

By now, the evolution of private pension plans in this country has progressed to the stage at which an entire generation of employees has been in them long enough to qualify for retirement pensions. They can be loosely considered our first generation of retirees, for most of them come from parents who did not retire. For one thing, prior generations did not live as long. As Warren Peterson points out, "For a large proportion of the population to live into advanced age is essentially a new phenomenon in history, a new experience in this century for American society."

Further, our fathers, no matter how long they lived, usually went on working until they died, could no longer find work, or could no longer perform it. Our mothers are even less likely to have formally retired, or to have had working careers to retire from. In this sense, we of today's generation lack role models and are engendering a new experience about which we have little valid information and less real understanding.

The problem is not a lack of books and articles on retirement; we are being flooded with them. But most of them echo one another, and few have anything to say that people with common sense do not already know. Preretirement planning and counseling is also very much in vogue these days in adult education courses and company training programs. Many of these courses are designed and conducted by employed people whose only knowledge of how retirement should be planned comes from books and articles and from the programs presented by their counterparts employed in other companies, other schools. An increasing proportion of the currently available advice and information about retirement is being supplied by people and organizations who are in the business of making retirement attractive and whose counsel is, as I shall point out, suspect.

These advisors depict retirement as the end result of a process of arranging, planning, calculating, and transacting, for which they provide a seemingly endless array of checklists and self-administered quizzes. The person engaged in this process plans a budget, reviews his medical and life insurance coverage, studies his employment benefits, his pension plan rights, his Social Security and Medicare benefits. He evaluates his assets, makes decisions on buying or selling his home, recreational vehicle, boat. He studies the cost of living, the climate and the facilities in his home community and in other possible communities, considers his estate, reviews his will, reorganizes his investments, consults his broker, his attorney, his accountant, his real estate agent, his tax advisor, his personnel manager, his doctor. He investigates hobbies, anticipates making some psychological adjustments, and plans how to spend his time and money.

All this is so sensible, practical, and thorough that he is misled into thinking that he understands retirement and is prepared for it. All these activities do constitute the *business of arranging* retirement, but almost none of it touches on the *experience of becoming* a retired person. That experience still remains so substantially hidden and private that it comes to each of us as though it were happening for the first time. To the extent that I think I have come to understand it, I will try to share it with you.

In doing so, I shall for the most part speak in generalities, avoiding statistics, case histories, and footnote references, which are the apparatus of the social scientist who is rightly required to quantify, objectify, and prove assertions. I do not intend to add to the already abundant literature of gerontology, even were I qualified to do so. My intention is to do just the opposite—to share common feelings and experiences with my peers who are approaching or entering retirement and to be subjective about them, to describe people and situations, not cases or statistics, to express attitudes as I heard, perceived, or understood them, to say what seemed to me to be happening to people, and to quote or paraphrase or interpret what some of them have said to me. I will try to be intuitive and empathic about their inner experiences—the opposite of the scientific attitude—because I am more concerned with shared feelings than with reported facts.

Because I believe the more important feelings are often those mostly deeply concealed and dimly seen, I will give great significance to the occasional glimpses of them I was given, and thus may draw important conclusions from what may seem to be scanty evidence.

During the years I was acquiring the material for this book, I was both an observer of and a participant in the retirement process, so I cannot now pretend to be an objective reporter. Our interior experiences, which are sometimes as much a mystery to us as they are to others, are always subjective, entirely unique, and, even when similar or identical to the experiences of others, they retain for us their special particularity.

Each of us constructs his own reality. And the observer is always part of the observation. The reality of retirement as I have observed it and will describe it is thus inescapably my own conception, filtered through my biases and experiences, my abilities and perceptions.

Others who see the same things will of course view and interpret them differently, or see things I do not. This is inevitable and for my purposes not important.

What is important to me is to hold up a mirror, however flawed or distorted, in which others may recognize some aspect of themselves. It is my hope that when and if they do, they will realize that they are not as separate and isolated, as different and out of step as they may have believed, that others share some of their secret thoughts and hidden feelings, that we are undergoing a common experience each of us need not invent separately, that we can learn from one another and help one another to reshape that experience into something far more enriching and gratifying than we can achieve alone. Perhaps together we can make a better path, or many new paths, for others to follow.

Chapel Hill, N.C.

Half the trouble in the world comes from people being cheerful when they should be concerned.

—SYDNEY J. HARRIS

I. HIDDEN FEELINGS, SECRET THOUGHTS

Some of the concealed feelings people have about imminent retirement, and how they react to the way they feel.

MEN WHO HOLD positions of authority and responsibility lead dual lives. One is lived in the business or professional world, the world of competition and striving, of power and achievement. The other is lived in the smaller, more private world of family life, the world of marriage, home, and children. It is to this world they retreat when the pressures of the other grow too strong. Indeed, the balance achieved in shifting one's weight between them often determines one's emotional stability. Whatever happens in either generally affects what happens in the other.

On retirement, we become permanent exiles from the world in which we have spent most of our waking hours and move completely into the smaller quarters of our private life, which we must consequently reorganize for continual occupancy. Throughout our adult lives we have occupied them only intermittently; now we know we shall never leave them again. We bring with us all the emotional baggage of a lifetime at work, baggage for which there does not seem to be a place, but which we must put down somewhere.

In these terms, we can recognize retirement to be a major life change with far-reaching consequences involving substantial adjustments. It can be seen as two separate but concurrent events: the ending of one world and the restructuring of the other. They can be better understood when considered separately, and I will start with the first, for we enter retirement by going through the terminal stage of working for a living.

This event can best be understood in the context of executive thinking, which has its own special imperatives. Every executive has learned as he progressed in his career that responsibility is not difficult to acquire; what is hard to get, what is essential for success, is authority, a word embracing many things all executives readily recognize without having to define. Primarily, authority is the power to reward or withhold, and thereby to influence, control, and direct the actions of others, to create and impose on them a value system of one's own, to make decisions they must accept and assign priorities they must respect. It is a heady kind of power, establishing one's place in the hierarchy of one's fellows and shaping all one's relationships.

No matter how else it may be construed, retirement is the total loss of authority, finally and completely. It hurts.

This hurt is something other than and something more than wounded pride. Every executive develops strong reflexes for protecting the authority he has acquired, and is psychologically tuned to be highly sensitive to any attack on it. Being stripped bare of all authority triggers inner warning signals that clamor a kind of red alert. The nervous system is flooded with a reflexive danger signal that is impossible to ignore. There is no shut-off switch for this alarm system. Part of the executive's adjustment to retirement consists in suppressing or learning to ignore that signal, as an amputee must learn to ignore the ghost pains in his severed limb.

"I was truly glad to be relieved of my responsibilities; over the years they had been getting heavier and I had been getting weary of carrying them on my back," a factory manager told me. "But when the weight was lifted," he continued, "instead of relief I felt anxiety. I kept telling myself how good it was that someone else was carrying the load, but what I felt was that something was terribly wrong. It was like waking up with a start from a nightmare I couldn't remember."

A high proportion of retirees has a hospital stay in the first year of retirement; some studies report a 90-percent chance of hospitalization in the first year. The causes vary widely, but almost always there is some sort of health crisis. I believe that this crisis is related in some way and is a physical response to an otherwise unanswered alarm signal that is clamoring in the nervous system.

The response to the alarm may take other forms. One is a great concentration at retirement on the business, the busy-ness, of retiring: an elaborate making of plans and investigating of all sorts of questions. Many of these plans are never carried out and in the course of time most of the questions prove unimportant or even irrelevant, but they seem to help alleviate the distress caused by the psychic alarm signal.

An industrial librarian described his experience with "busy-ness": "Having lived and worked in New York City all my life, I thought it would be good to spend my retirement years in a small town with a pollution-free environment. When I started studying weather and pollution patterns, I realized this was not going to be an easy problem to solve—polluted air generated in one place moves with the winds

25

and air currents for hundreds of miles. I started reading up on it and sending for reports from government agencies and weather bureaus, and as retirement became imminent I began to visit some of the Environmental Protection Agency offices and talking to the professionals. The more I learned, the more complex the problem became, and I spent months delving deeper and deeper into the whole problem and building up a whole library of technical data. I finally narrowed my search to four communities, and then it turned out that none of them was the kind I would like to live in. The place I finally chose was one I could have selected at random in the first place; it was pretty much at the national average in pollution."

It does not require the actual loss of authority to set off the alarm; the threat of it is enough. The knowledge that retirement is coming up constitutes such a threat and often generates anxiety about it. This tends to result in an intense focusing upon a particular problem which then assumes an importance far out of all proportion.

One couple spent their final preretirement year living uncomfortably in temporary quarters solely to reduce their state income tax; every decision they made during that year was determined by its effect upon their state tax. Nothing seemed more important at that time. They did reduce the tax somewhat, but the fact was that the tax was just not that important, and paying it would really not have been much of a hardship—indeed, no hardship at all.

In another instance, two years before retirement a friend of mine became preoccupied with the view of a small lake from the picture window in her living room. Some of the window framing, interrupting the view, bothered her so much that she spent the better part of two years working on the problem of how to replace the windows. It was a major subject of conversation with visitors, and she had a stream of salesmen and contractors in to give estimates and make suggestions. Most of her generalized anxieties about retirement were funneled into this problem of the view from the picture window.

For one man, the focus became the sale price of his home. He decided arbitrarily on a particular figure and would not come down a single penny. The most important thing was to sell the house for the exact figure he had set. He spent more than six months negotiating and bargaining with agents and prospective buyers, working up a genuine crisis as time began to run short and concentrating all his energies on the sale of the house while neglecting all the other matters that needed his attention. The fact was that a few thousand dollars more or less would not have made the slightest difference in his situation. But he was able to use the issue as an outlet for his anxiety and as a way of responding to his inner sense of alarm.

As I think back on the various issues that were used for this purpose, none of which was really worth the time and trouble devoted to it, it becomes clear that they were all "safe" problems; they seem unconsciously to have been chosen precisely *because the practical outcome did not greatly matter.* In other words, there was a certain amount of security to be gained in piling all one's anxiety on a single issue, if that issue were not really crucial, if failure would result in no substantial injury.

If we can accept the repeated occurrences of this kind of behavior as being in any way typical or as part of the retirement syndrome, we can make some hypotheses about it, particularly relating to the secrecy about which I have re-marked. What seems to happen when a "safe" problem is used—or created—as the focus for a generalized anxiety, is that it disguises the causes of that anxiety. Indeed, it dis-guises them both from the person who feels anxious and from those around him. Because the subject of concern appears to be so specific and highly focused, it makes it possible to avoid recognizing that there is a generalized anxiety and thus forestalls any investigation of the real cause.

Other factors are also at work to promote self-deception. An executive nearing retirement is like a public official whose term is expiring and who cannot run again. He is a lame duck. The fact that there is a known time limit on his authority and influence is a restriction on the amount of authority and influence he can exert today. His potential exit from the scene becomes a factor in the calculations of others caught up in the same game, both foes and allies. His power is diminished because his value as an ally is nearing an end and his opponents know he will soon leave the field.

No executive adroit enough to have attained power and influence in the first place would be unaware of the importance of playing down or altogether concealing his potential retirement. This is a quite conscious tactic. If there is any one thing all executives learn, it is how to conceal the places where they can be attacked, where they may be vulnerable to loss of power. In time, this becomes an automatic reflex, part of the conditioned response to any threat to authority.

What accompanies it, however, is an extension of concealment: What one hides from others is more easily concealed from oneself, particularly if it is a thought one would rather not entertain. The actor can easily become lost in the role. So there is a process of subtle denial, intended to deceive others but which one can also use to deceive oneself.

Perhaps this is the reason that future retirement has no more reality to most executives than a long-term business forecast; it is an imagined and hypothetical event. This may also explain why so many executives work full and heavy schedules right up to the moment they are due in the president's office for the little get-together marking the opening ceremonies of formal retirement. Simone de Beauvoir and others have remarked on the odd phenomenon of the employee who has known for years the date on which he will retire, but who is astonished when it arrives; it comes as a surprise.

It may all derive from that peculiar capacity we seem to have, of knowing a thing without believing it. An example is the familiar dictum of all business organizations: No one is indispensable. All executives know this to be so and do not find it upsetting to acknowledge it. But what is incredible, unthinkable, is the realization at retirement that we are *actually being dispensed with.*

This resembles our attitude about dying. We all know we are mortal and are not distressed to acknowledge our mortality. At the same time we do not really believe in it as a present event—only as a future one. In the same sense, retirement is always seen as a future event, not as a present one.

When we realize that retirement is imminent or actually at hand, it is hard to contemplate calmly that the things for which we are responsible will hereafter be tended to by someone else. In the picture drawn by people who have not themselves had the experience of it, this realization is described as resulting in a loss of self-esteem, or of status, but in my view there is a far more important and more carefully concealed result: It raises the entire question of whether we were essential in the first place. How important could we have been in the scheme of things, if these things can readily get along without us? In a subtle way, this is a rehearsal of our own death and a humiliating lesson in mortality, the lesson being that when we are subtracted from it, the universe seems to be undiminished.

Again, this is the kind of revelation we tend to conceal

29

from others and, in doing so, from ourselves. It is unwanted self-knowledge; so we look away from it and focus on something else instead.

What we try to focus on, for our own comfort, is achievement. When we near retirement we are able for the first time to know the whole story of our career, for its last stage is almost completed. We have spent all our working lives creating our own personal history, our eyes fixed on the future consequences of our acts and decisions. There has always been a next stage in our careers, the events of which we are formulating in the present: the next job assignment, pay adjustment, promotion, or job change. But now for the first time we have reached the place where our history stops; there is no next stage.

For the first time, we can measure the entire distance from where we started a lifetime ago to the farthest place we have reached. We can also measure the distance between the targets at which we aimed and the ones we actually hit, between the hopes and the actuality, between the amount of striving and the extent of fulfillment.

It never comes out exactly right, of course; there is always a gap. Our lives never accord exactly with our intentions; whatever we set out to do is reshaped day by day. But as long as the action continued, we could strive to affect the outcome. When one comes to retirement, this can no longer be done. The action is over, time has run out, and the outcome has finally been fixed.

The time now is not for action, but for judgment. When at last we can look at the total work of our lifetime, we must ask ourselves: What did I accomplish? And that leads to: Was it worth a lifetime of effort to accomplish it? And because all executives who have attained power have had to compete with others for it: How did I come out in the competition?

We can all recall much of which we can be proud, specific instances that provide reassuring evidence that our work has indeed had some meaning. But even as we look back and think, "This was good," we know it is over and already part of the past. The effects of our work may perhaps endure, but our part in them has been or will be forgotten. On the other hand, we cannot fail to see that much of what we did was written on water; it no longer makes any difference. The issues of policy, procedure, and principle about which we consider ourselves to have been the champions have already been won, or lost, or compromised. It is painful to recognize that most of them no longer really matter; time and events have moved on to other issues and left these behind. Even the victories, the contributions that are credited to us, are no longer very important to anyone else; we realize that no other person cares about them as much as we do.

Thus, retirement transforms a world in which there was not only an active present, but also a meaningful past and a pregnant future, into a world in which there is no present and no future. It has become a recollection and ceased to be an experience. And we realize that the battles, crises, and great decisions in which we participated have not really become history. They are simply our own personal memories.

This transformation has the effect of somehow lessening the value of whatever it is we have spent our life on—and it does so precisely at the time we need assurances of our own value.

The sense of it was best expressed to me by a man who estimated that the work he had done in the preceding six or seven years had been erased—nullified by time, by subsequent events, and by others who followed after him. He believed that very few executives can influence the course of affairs more than two or three years into the future. So the effective span of control, the period in which one's influence can be discerned, he calculated as a floating time range of about seven years, five behind and two ahead. This range moves forward year after year. As one comes within a couple of years of retirement, the future portion begins diminishing to zero, and five years or so after retirement the entire time period of a man's influence on his working world "moves right off the screen."

For himself, he told me, "It made me feel as though I was being erased from history. In a way, it is another way to die."

And, of course, at retirement the final scores are posted on the lifelong competition in the success game. The game plan, the strategy of career management, was to gain the greatest amount of success, but success is always relative, never absolute. One measures success only by comparison with others and in comparison with one's expectations.

But the race, the competition, is never over until someone crosses the finish line (a good synonym for retirement) when the relative order of finish and the final payout are unalterably established.

This is the way men pass judgment on themselves: "George and I joined the Three M Company the same year. Three years before I retired, he was made a vice-president. I never got that far, I'm sorry to say. I don't know why—I always thought I was better than George, but evidently I failed to convince management. And evidently George's strategy paid off better than mine."

Another man said, "My boss at Avon always told me that I was making a mistake when I quit to go to Max Factor. Whenever we met afterward, we'd half-kid each other about who was being proved right. I finally got to a level at Factor that was higher than my former boss'. In effect, I outranked him, something I could never have done if I had stayed under him. By the time I retired, he had freely conceded that my strategy had worked better than his and that he probably would have been better off if he had changed jobs as I did."

Looking back, another executive confided, "I still remember what agony Jane and I went through trying to decide whether or not I should accept the company's offer to transfer me to another division in an entirely different capacity. We stayed up far into the night trying to read the future, figuring the advantages and liabilities, whether or not I would progress faster, whether it was a good career move for me. We finally decided the change made sense, and I said yes. Now that I know how it came out, I realize it was the turning point in my career and I would never have been as successful staying where I was."

A divisional controller told me, "I've never said this to anyone before, not even my wife, but I feel I could have and should have gone farther than I did. I can see now that I was much too cautious, afraid to take chances, so that I let a lot of good opportunities go by. I'm sorry I didn't listen to a former boss of mine, who gave me this advice: 'If you're going to strike out, at least do it swinging at the ball; don't be struck out standing at the plate with your bat on your shoulder.' It was good advice; I wish I had listened."

And finally this judgment: "There were four of us who came in around the same time in a drastic change of management. We were considered the new management team, and eventually we did turn the company around. But of the original four, I was the least successful in terms of earnings, status, and authority, even though we were always referred to as equals, as The Four Horsemen. I was just as good as the others in what I did, but they proved to be smarter than me in getting rewards."

Was it all worthwhile?

We cannot avoid making some kind of judgment on the question of whether it was all worth doing, whether we have spent our lives wisely and to good purpose. "Looking back," an executive told me, "it's hard for me to convince myself that a life spent in the service of a shoe manufacturer can be fully justified. It was a way of making a living, supporting a family, educating the kids, and assuring financial security—all good purposes, I'm sure—but maybe I could have served those purposes doing some other kind of work, in a way that would have more meaning than making profits for the family that owned the shoe company. I don't really know what I mean—it's just that I'd hate to have it written on my tombstone how I spent my life. Yet I can't tell you what's wrong with it—or that it wasn't worthwhile."

At this time of judgment, the analogy with dying often surfaces, sometimes in contexts I could not anticipate. Most people would agree that the currency of executive power is the ability to make and enforce a decision, to state and protect a principle, to institute and enact a policy. In this sense, every executive, everyone with authority in the business world, is engaged in continual combat with other decisions, other principles, other policies. What happens to them when we leave the field and are no longer there to protect and defend them? They stand alone, and without us there is no way to secure them. We can put memoranda in the files, enjoin others to stand fast, and leave instructions no one is compelled to obey. But we know that we cannot prevent our work from being reshaped or even discarded by strangers.

"It is something like dying," a man said to me. "With this difference: I can leave a will stating my wishes and disposing of my estate and have confidence that others will be obligated to do as I say. But at retirement there is no way of leaving a will, my managerial principles cannot be left to anyone, and no one has any obligation to respect my last wishes."

At retirement, then, a number of reactions are taking place at the same time: the recapitulation of a lifetime career, the final judgments on it, and the subtle devaluing of it. In addition to these, there is a process that is almost never spoken about but that is equally grave. This is the giving up of the career goals one has striven for but not attained.

What a man has not yet accomplished, he now must concede, he will never accomplish. The play is over, the game ended, the scenario completed, and time has run out.

One cannot overestimate the trauma of giving up unattained goals; a person facing retirement can scarcely do so except by diminishing their importance. This is another part of the process of diminishment that occurs at a time when we are feeling stripped bare of so many other attributes important to us.

The kinds of feelings I have described have one characteristic in common: They are without a clear focus. They are not directed toward or at anyone, not even oneself; they are diffused. They may more properly be described as states of mind or attitudes, for they have no built-in dynamics and do not lead to action. What is being described here seems to be a condition, a trauma, an invisible wound.

A person in whom these feelings are swirling has been psychologically injured and is to a great extent unaware of it. To the extent that he is aware, there seems to be nothing he can do about it.

People in such a situation find it important to preserve as much normalcy as possible; they go about their usual business in their usual way, pretending to everyone and to themselves that nothing has happened, but aware of an inner turbulence that must be carefully controlled. And it is this, too, that contributes to the secrecy in which feelings about retirement are cloaked—to all outward appearances nothing unusual is going on.

This kind of deception is self-perpetuating. Few of us, in the years before our retirement, have any idea that our associates who retire are going through any significant kind of inner experience. When our time comes and we feel emotional distress, we try to repress and conceal it because we consider it to be an inappropriate response, and we attribute it to personal weakness, some fault or failing in ourselves. Thus, we in turn become deceptive role models for those who follow us.

II. MYTHS AND REALITIES

How retirement myths are created and perpetuated by people who can profit from them, and some of the realities they conceal.

AS RETIREMENT BECOMES more widely experienced, I believe it will be better understood and the kinds of emotional stress it engenders will be more openly displayed, more readily accepted, and more sensibly managed. But misconceptions persist, and one reason, I believe, is that "retirement" has become a field of professional expertise, described and defined by social scientists, psychologists, and other professionals, who see it as an aspect of gerontology and who link retirement strongly to aging. They tend to see the retired person as an old person and retirement as simply an event in the course of growing old. This leads to the tendency to consider reactions to retirement as being age-specific.

From this angle of vision, retirement as an experience separate from aging is seen only peripherally and sometimes not seen at all. From this view, strong messages are generated: To retire is to acknowledge that you have become an old person; therefore, you have acquired the characteristics you have learned to associate with old people; whatever your problems, they arise not so much from your retirement as from your aging. All this helps unwittingly to foster the

37

myths about retirement and to divert attention from retirement, the experience over which we can exercise a good deal of autonomy and direction, and turn it instead toward aging, over which we have much less control. This distinction is important: Whereas aging is innate and inevitable, retirement is neither.

Researchers study people in groups and tend to speak in the language of statistics. And they speak primarily to one another. When they do, they employ a professional shorthand, in which emotions I have described are referred to by such bloodless but familiar terms as "role loss" and "lowered self-esteem." In the course of objectifying, quantifying, and categorizing a human experience, subtleties are necessarily lost; the vague, the ineffable, and the indescribable must be omitted, and what is concluded may be accurate without being true, may represent the experience yet omit the essence of it, which is the humanity of the person whose experience it was.

Few people who retire ever get to read the experts' studies and reports, so it cannot be said that they are deceived or misinformed by them. But these studies and reports provide the raw material for what is then fleshed out, dramatized, and simplified—that is to say, distorted—in the more popular books and articles, which perpetuate the misconceptions. From time to time, professionals invited to address classes on retirement planning lecture on what their studies have shown about retirement, but they generally recast their findings into more acceptable, reassuring, nonthreatening forms in keeping with the well-meaning but mistaken convention of not "upsetting the patient."

I have heard a widely respected professional assure a class of people preparing for retirement that there is nothing they have to fear. He put a list of "typical fears" on the blackboard: fear of loneliness, fear of poverty, fear of sickness, fear of death, fear of diminished mental capacity. Ticking them off one by one, he explained that with retirement villages and nursing homes older people can always be with others, with Social Security they are assured of always having an income, with improved medical care and facilities they will get better treatment than their parents did, they do live longer and in some respects even improve their capacities. In support of the last, he cited an experiment in measuring "vigilance," which showed that older people were better at pressing a button in response to random blips on a screen than younger people, who tended more quickly to be bored and become inattentive—and therefore less "vigilant." His reassurance was well-meant, I am certain, as was his assumption that the best thing to do for people who are retiring is to reassure them.

But even these professionals do not go as far as the writers of articles and advertisements for the "over fifties." They depict both retirement and aging as opportunities. Because the increasing numbers of older and retired people constitute a growing market in our consumer society, these ads and articles offer them all sorts of opportunities to *do*—and, in order to do, to *buy*. They point out that age and leisure create both the need and the opportunity to acquire, despite the less heralded fact that retirees are at a time of life when it is generally more sensible to dispose of rather than accumulate possessions.

Myths about retirement are fed by all the people with strong commercial incentives to perpetuate them: those who sell the mobile homes, recreational vehicles, cruises, golf carts, and retirement acreage on lake fronts. They are aided by those who sell access to such things: investment advice, stock brokerage, insurance annuities, banking services, travel tours, and Sun Belt condominiums.

Inspirational and advertising copy writers are chiefly responsible for the popular and familiar image of retirement:

the rosy-cheeked couple in the canoe, waving from the deck of a cruise ship, or riding the fairway in a golf cart. Occasionally, she is seen smiling at us from under a straw hat, gardening beside a cheery mobile home, while he, pipe in mouth, comes up the path with his string of fish. In this fantasy world, the population consists entirely of long and happily married, gray-haired couples; there are no widows or widowers, no late-life divorces, and no lonely people. In this fantasy, there is no sickness, people do not use crutches or wheelchairs. They are always well dressed and constantly engaged in some leisure or recreational activity well within their means. But most of all, they are smiling and happy.

Inspirational writers also offer impossible role models. They are fond of holding up Grandma Moses and Pablo Casals as people I might emulate in some way. They point out that Tintoretto painted "Paradise" at eighty, Titian "The Battle of Lepanto" at ninety-eight, and that Tennyson wrote "Crossing the Bar" at eighty-three. They seem to think this news should reassure me, but it only serves to confirm how extraordinary these people were and how different from me. It is also commonplace to refer to obscure people ("seventy-eight-year-old grandmother"), who do such things as sky diving or mountain climbing. These writers tell of people who have gone back to high school or college or who study auto mechanics, weaving, or pottery. Some even point admiringly to clever but ordinary folks who carve elves from corncobs, laminate autumn leaves in plastic, and do other things "for fun and profit." Again, these people are all happy.

But perhaps the most powerful of the myth makers are the newest, the members of the profession that sprang up everywhere in the late seventies and that has seized jurisdiction over the entire subject of planned retirement. These are the preretirement counselors, whose commercial organizations design, sell, and administer preretirement planning programs for the larger companies. (Employees of smaller companies that do not offer such counseling have access to similar courses these counselors also design for adult education programs.)

A single article in *The New York Times* illustrates the function preretirement "professionals" perform in the business world. " 'This is a real growth field,' said Clif Fichtner, director of AIM (Action for Independent Maturity), a subsidiary of the American Association for Retired Persons [and a major supplier of retirement planning programs to leading companies]. . . . "While concern for their departing employees' welfare is one reason . . ." the *Times* observes, "altruism is not the only motivation for companies to add [preretirement counseling] to existing benefits."

The article quotes Roger O'Meara, who did a major study of retired people for the Conference Board, a business research organization: " 'If an employee is reluctant to retire, it can cause morale and productivity problems among other employees as well.' " The *Times* notes that the 1979 federal legislation raising the mandatory retirement age to seventy has "forced many companies to confront the prospect of an aging and increasingly stagnant work force. Retirement counseling is seen as a possible alternative."

Dr. Edward Fitzpatrick, director of the Industry Consortium Retirement Planning Program at the National Council on Aging, explained, "It's kind of like inducing retirement. . . . Companies would like to have their employees know what they can expect in retirement, so they'll be willing to leave. . . ."

Thus, the so-called professionals and the employer companies join forces to present to older employees "what they can expect in retirement" in a way that will "induce retirement," "make them willing to leave," and "overcome the employee's reluctance to retire." I find it difficult to see this

41

kind of "counseling" as objective, disinterested, and unbiased.

When the skills of the corporate propagandist, with the aid of the paid "expert," are directed toward inducing the employee to leave, and to go without making a fuss, it is extremely difficult for him to challenge the myth of tranquil, happy retirement without sounding like the sour, negative, aging malcontent the same professionals warn against becoming.

Some employees are naive, I'm sure, but generally the successful executive, who has spent his lifetime in the business world, knows when he is being manipulated. This explains why, according to the same *Times* article, many resist attending the counseling programs: "According to Alexander Hood, director of staff development for Time Inc., 'It's extremely difficult to get employees to consider retirement counseling,' " and according to Paul Torres, manager of specialized training at Con Edison, " 'There's a stigma, particularly among people in management; they're afraid if they come to the program they won't get a promotion because the company will think they're just waiting for retirement.' "

A friend who sent me a clipping of this article wrote, "Does this fellow think people enrolled in company retirement programs actually are candidates for promotion in that company? He must be kidding."

But I don't think it is simply fear of becoming unpromotable that keeps executives from taking company retirement counseling. The ones who have discussed it with me agree that there are two compelling reasons. The first, which I have mentioned, is the fact that identifying oneself as preparing for retirement is to become a lame duck, to diminish one's power and authority. The other, which I have tried to substantiate, is that the company is serving its own purposes more faithfully, perhaps, than it serves the interests of the employee, and it does not require much cynicism to recognize this, just sound business intuition.

This kind of intuition was expressed to me with an added insight: "It's not that they want me to have a happy retirement, as they say. Nor just that they want to get me on the retirement track and to make it seem like a good thing to do, so that I'll be more inclined to do it. It's also that they are washing their hands of whatever might turn out badly. In effect, they are telling me, 'We want to show you how to go about it, how to do it right and avoid all the mistakes and pitfalls. Then, if you don't listen to our advice, whatever happens will be your own fault. But even if you do listen to our advice, whatever goes wrong will be no fault of ours— it will be due to the fact that you didn't follow our advice or didn't do it right. We will always be able to say we did the best we could and the rest was up to you.' "

"What's wrong with that?" I asked this man.

"What's wrong," he replied, "is the implicit assumption that a successful retirement is simply a matter of making the right arrangements and having the right attitudes, that there is nothing to fear, that it is something anyone can manage with just a little common sense."

I have not yet met a man who ever told the personnel officer his real reason for avoiding the retirement program, and when I asked why, I was told, "Look, when you're getting ready to retire, it's the wrong time to start making enemies in the personnel department. They're the ones who present the program, but they're also the ones who handle your benefits and your pension and all the other important things, and they are the ones you have to work with to straighten anything out after you've left the company. So you just don't start making waves."

There is still one more reason for shunning retirement

advice from the company: "The most attractive part of retirement to me is the fact that once I'm out, the company can't run my life any longer or tell me what to do. The last thing I want to hear from the company is how they think I should manage my affairs when I retire."

And finally, "The fact is, like most responsible adults, I've managed my own affairs most of my life. I really don't need to be told that it's important to make a will or how to buy or sell a house or make a budget or manage my money. And if I wanted advice about any of those things, I'd go to my own advisors, not to the company, to get it."

It is hard to define to what extent thinking about retirement constitutes planning it, because so much of our thinking about retirement, aside from money, is so vague.

Those who seek advice and those who don't, those who think about the way of life they will follow in retirement and those who don't, those who study the subject and those who don't, may all have one thing in common: that they do not really have a plan. Information, yes; possibilities, perhaps; financial provisions, very likely; biases and opinions, certainly. But not a plan.

Some men simply don't want to think about it. "I'll deal with it when the time comes." "I'm not going to worry about it." "I've got more important things on my mind right now." "I'll just play it by ear."

Others deny the need: "What's there to plan? How to sit around and play checkers?" "I can always find something to do; I'll keep busy somehow." And even, "They'll have to push me—I certainly don't intend to jump."

The most deceptive are those who conceal the subject, like Poe's purloined letter, in plain view: "The thing I'm going to do," the assistant school principal told me, "is open a hardware store somewhere, a kind of fixit shop. I love gadgets and tools, all that stuff. All I'll need is a partner who knows how to run the store and some way I can get away every couple of months to do all the traveling my wife and I want to do; I wouldn't want to be tied down." Thus, he was able to get planning out of the way with a "plan" that was no more than a fantasy.

Rejecting the retirement myths we are offered is one thing. It is quite another to know what retirement is really like. So the executive retiring these days finds it hard to visualize himself as a retired person and, in the absence of a variety of possible behaviors and valid role models, has to invent his own concept of himself in retirement.

Creativity along these lines is necessarily limited; a person has to start at some familiar point, and his imagination often does not venture far from it. Thus, many of the retirement concepts people do invent come to resemble the very myths, fantasies, and stereotypes they are designed to replace.

I have in mind two major executives, one from IBM, the other from DuPont, both hardheaded, no-nonsense people. Yet the first retired to spend his time yacht racing, the other to devote himself to his golf game. Neither plan worked; what is surprising is that these men expected their plans to work and were taken aback when they did not. What can this tell us?

First, when it comes to inventing a way of life in retirement, the most sensible and practical of people can and do pursue fantasies—or mistake fantasy for reality. It seems to me that this happens because the line between fantasy and reality is blurred, and this blurring occurs where the light of experience is too dim for clarity. People pursuing their business careers have practically no contact with retired people; the brief glimpses they may have are almost always distorted.

The distortion is reinforced because it is very important to a retired man to demonstrate to the former associates he left behind that he has done a good job of planning his retirement, that the plan is working well, that he is as successful in retirement as the other is in his career. The competitive spirit does not die when retirement comes. When he visits his former company, he wants to be envied, not pitied, so he makes sure to emphasize all of the fantasy aspects of his way of life that he knows will generate the greatest envy. Thus he, too, perpetuates the myth of the carefree retiree.

After retirement, links with former business associates are very soon broken, so that they rarely learn the sequel to the story of the enviable retirement. They take it for granted that Jack has gone on yacht racing and that somewhere Tom, when they think of him, is still improving his golf handicap. If they checked later, they would learn that yacht racing just didn't do it for Jack and that three years after retiring he sold his yacht and began to look around for something to do. Perhaps they never learn that Tom sold his town house at the edge of the fairway and moved to a university town where he is helping administer a volunteer social service agency. Neither Jack nor Tom refers to his first version of retirement as a mistake; they tend to describe it as "getting it out of my system." What they got out of their systems was the myth of retirement as a perpetual holiday.

An additional way of accounting for the tendency to fantasize a retirement life-style is to see it as an antidote to the vague tensions and anxieties that arise at retirement. As compensation for unrealized goals, it is perhaps not surprising that one promises oneself real rewards that once were only fantasies: a life of nothing but pleasure.

To offset all that he is losing, and somehow quench the doubts and fears that arise when he becomes aware of feelings he does not understand, cannot describe, and is unable to resolve, the retired executive plunges into the process of planning a new life for himself. Working with unfamiliar materials, he tries to shape a way of life that, for him, still seems unreal.

46

It is not surprising, then, that his product reflects the unreality.

But, more than that, his ability to think things out efficiently is severely limited, for, precisely at the time he turns to consider his unshaped future, he is like an electric appliance after the plug has been pulled. He has become a deactivated mechanism: There is a zero reading on the dials that used to measure his productivity, potential for further achievement, career progress, his influence, authority, and responsibility. This is the worst of all possible times for creating a sensible action program, and the process of doing so is itself a wounding experience. For the first time he begins to think of himself (to continue the machine analogy) not in terms of the functions he can perform, but of the salvage value of his parts.

He must ask himself what parts of himself can be saved and enlarged to fill the empty spaces; what skills can be adapted to other purposes, what knowledge or experience can be reshaped and redirected. Whatever he cannot use to build a new mechanism will be junked.

Here again, he must experience a kind of psychological wounding, an overthrow of his entire value system, the discarding of vital parts of his own identity, most particularly the parts that have given him value to himself. To accept the fact that they are now forever useless is psychologically in a class with suicide and self-mutilation, except that they are entirely interior experiences, generally unobserved and unknown to anyone else.

The stock in trade of most executives, the tools with which they carved out successful careers, consists of certain skills—primarily judgmental skills, the carefully and painfully developed capacity to be right more often than wrong. It also includes experience—a firsthand knowledge of the terrain that comes from having traversed it, or a variation of it, some time before. It also includes memory, or history—an understanding of the way things came to be as they are and of the hidden forces that have moved them into a particular configuration. And, often underestimated, it always includes a carefully built network of significant relationships, a structure of enormous complexity that must be as constantly tended as a spider tends its web and that has determined where one is placed in relation to all the significant others, both in one's own organization and in the trade, occupation, or profession as a whole. It is made of alliances of fluctuating degrees of reliability, potential, and promise, of relationships based on equality and shared interests, as well as the unequal relationships with those above and below, in a constantly shifting hierarchy. Perhaps more than anything else it is the skill of finding the optimum but ever-changing line between one's own career goals and the objectives of the organization one serves.

At retirement, when these skills have brought a man to the point of his maximum attainment, when he is reaping the dividends that could have come only from longevity in the use of his abilities, they must all be discarded. There is no way in which he can use them any longer. And this leaves him with the awful question: Without them, what am I?

Very few of us, no matter how long we have lived, know ourselves well enough to be certain that we have any worth aside from what we know and what we do. Even if we are certain, we have never had to put that confidence to the test. But, to a man who has devoted a lifetime to developing and using his career skills, the idea of abandoning them forever seems inevitably linked to the idea of self-diminishment. He has no foundation for imagining himself to be able to exist as a whole and functioning person outside the social and psychological world in which he made his career. For that matter, he has little evidence that there is a world outside it for him to function in. He has been so thoroughly imbedded in his business or professional culture that it fills his known universe; he can theorize about other cultures—about the culture of retirement particularly—but this is only speculation. People who can readily visualize themselves as students, as husbands, or as fathers are unable to form a clear mental image of themselves as retirees; the picture is much too shadowy.

So there is a strong tendency to fill the void with almost any sort of goal, however arbitrary or poorly thought out, the idea being not so much to achieve it as, by establishing it, to give one an air of purpose and direction. The need for these things is strong and finds its expression in busy-ness, preoccupation with the making of plans and arrangements, investigation of all sorts of technical questions, and pinning down of details. A man in this state does not give the impression, as one might expect, of winding down his affairs. Quite the contrary, he acts like a man accelerating rather than slowing; he is wrapped in a dense cloud of business that needs attending to.

The dismantling of the social structure of his business life is generally far greater than he ever anticipated, because he has rarely if ever had to realize how deeply integrated with it he has been and how much support it has been giving him. As with the experience of gravity, we rarely realize how profoundly it has been acting on us until we are released from it. And when we are, the world turns topsy-turvy.

In the situation he is about to enter at retirement, a man is at the very lowest point at which he is capable of planning a future. He cannot visualize it, his data are too scanty and too unreliable, and he is probably feeling loss, self-doubt, and psychic diminishment. His rational and analytical skills are unsuitable for the introspective and intuitive thinking he must do; it is a task for which he has no real understanding and in which he gets little assistance. He is undergoing a windstorm of unexpected and undeciphered feelings to which he does not know how to respond.

He can scarcely be blamed if he sketches a fantasy world and then attempts to live in it, if, in a way, he loses touch with his own reality.

I have offered some explanations of why many executives, particularly successful ones, consider retirement to be unreal, why they are surprised when confronted by it and shocked by the strong gusts of feelings it brings. It may explain why they are reluctant to discuss it and expose their vulnerability to others and angry when others come close to their uncomfortable secret. Although it is a private experience they are unable and unwilling to share, it is too painful and burdensome to shoulder alone. At this juncture, many men turn to their wives, the only person in their lives to whom most men feel free to express their fears and anxieties.

It is then that a man may discover the second part of the process of retirement, the changes it requires in his personal life, and the crisis it makes for his wife.

III. IMPACT ON THE MARRIAGE PARTNER

A man's retirement profoundly affects his wife and his marriage in ways they may not understand.

IT IS RARELY acknowledged how strongly a man's retirement affects his wife and how the impact on each affects their relationship. The tendency is to view the husband as the one being uprooted and his wife as being substantially unaffected by his retirement except, if she is a housewife, for the nuisance of having him at home and underfoot too much of the time. This trivializes some profound problems.

Cartoons and situation comedies make fun of the bumbling husband sitting around with nothing to do, interfering with his wife who is busy with her household chores and social activities. They see humor in the spectacle of the husband messing up the kitchen making his own lunch or reorganizing his wife's daily routine "for greater efficiency." But when these situations occur, they illustrate the plight of sensible people whose ordered world is being distorted for reasons they do not quite comprehend, in ways they could not anticipate.

If retirement is considered as a new life-stage for the man who is retiring—as I think it must—it has to be a new life-stage for his wife as well; whether or not she welcomes it, it is thrust upon her. Retirement is so entire a readjustment of his life that it must encompass the person with whom he shares his life; there is no way he can spare her as though it were an event in his life rather than in theirs; there is no way she can respond as though he were having another bad time at the office and she must simply nurse him through it. No, she is as much involved in his retirement as he is—and as threatened and as vulnerable, though in different ways.

Whether she is a housewife or a working wife who "runs the house," her domain is seriously threatened when her home and kitchen are intruded upon by anyone, and no less if the invader is her husband. In some cases, perhaps more, for as his full weight shifts into the home, she feels the sudden pressure upon her space, her autonomy, and her privacy, and there is no way she can entirely withstand it.

Consider her state of mind. She may not entirely realize or fully understand what is happening to her husband, but she certainly knows that he is being deeply affected by the ending of his career, and she probably senses that it is affecting him more deeply than either of them had expected.

At this juncture, his are the pressing needs, and she is expected to be the responding partner. She must collaborate with him in reorganizing his lifelong daily routine, adjusting the ways they spend and save, perhaps moving out of their accustomed community, restructuring their social life. Nonetheless, the moment for her to assume this role, whether she is a housewife or a career woman, could not be less propitious.

In the case of a working wife, some practical problems are visible in advance. If his retirement involves their moving elsewhere, this would require her to give up her job. Even if they do not relocate, his retirement often means her job stands in the way of such commonplace retirement plans as traveling leisurely and taking up new daytime activities together.

The retirement timetable, which must somehow be negotiated, raises such questions as: Does the wife intend to give up her career when her husband ends his? Does she want to? "I always assumed that was the sensible thing to do," a woman told me, "but when I saw for myself how upsetting and traumatic retirement was for Al, I had second thoughts. I didn't want to go through what was happening to him."

In this case, when Ann decided against taking early retirement, she faced the problem of working out a practical relationship between a working wife and a retired husband —which was in a way a reversal of their roles at the start of the marriage. Could they successfully make that turnaround? Not easily—but no matter how these things work out, it seems inescapable that the relationship will be reshaped in the process.

By way of contrast, consider the working wife who very much wanted to give up her job when her husband retired. But his calculations showed that they could maintain their living standard after his retirement only if her income continued. Besides, since she was younger by several years, her retirement benefits would be substantially diminished by early retirement. Nevertheless, she felt it unfair that she should now become the sole wage earner while her husband became "a man of leisure." It was a problem with many inner conflicts— between love and money, comfort and sacrifice, and the willingness to give happiness to the other at some cost to oneself. Regardless of the outcome, it is obvious that their relationship could not continue unchanged.

Even the prospect of a husband's retirement can be threatening to a wife; long before it actually occurs it can produce a vague foreboding, an undefined apprehension, for which some women feel some private guilt.

"I didn't want to think about it, and we never seemed to talk about it, but sometimes when Dick went off to work I'd wonder what it would be like when he began staying home and how different everything would be then. When I tried to visualize what would be different, I'd get a kind of blur. I was not sure that *different* meant *better*, that changing would be an improvement. There were many things I didn't want to change, that I liked exactly as they were, but thinking this way seemed selfish or disloyal or narrow-minded. When I began to disapprove of my own feelings, I would just put the whole thing out of my mind."

The point is that whether a woman is a housewife or has a career, her husband's retirement forces change upon her. She may be expected to give up a home that has been her life's work or leave a community in which she has won a place for herself. Just when she is able to see how deeply her husband is affected by the loss of his career, he may be asking her to give up a position that was hard to get and possibly irreplaceable and enter what amounts to a forced retirement. There is always the question of whether and to what extent she is willing to go along with or without protest or resentment. These are hard decisions to make, and marriages have foundered on them.

Negotiating the way in which each will adapt to the changed situation is a highly complex and difficult transaction. Certainly many couples bring it to a successful conclusion. But more often than is generally recognized, this negotiation ends in partial or even total failure, or in an imposed solution whereby one wins at the expense of the other. Perfectly evenhanded solutions rarely emerge as neatly as we would like them to.

One need not be especially discerning to see the great potential for trouble in the situation of a man undergoing a considerable amount of psychological turbulence, because his retirement is imminent, who turns to his wife for emotional support at the time she, too, is feeling threatened, vulnerable, and apprehensive. Although their emotions may be similar, their secret feelings and private thoughts are not, for to some

54

extent *their apprehensions are about each other.*

These concerns strain the fabric of marriage, putting pressure on its weakest threads, testing the relationship where it is most vulnerable. The points of rupture often seem to have no relationship to the subject of retirement—they may have to do with selfishness or sharing or caring, areas which may have taken years of careful stitching to produce a patch that will hold, places that both partners have learned to avoid straining. This awareness of a renewed vulnerability to each other, whether it comes slowly or suddenly, is especially disturbing in the later years after having been so carefully quieted long before.

"It is a feeling very much like jealousy," a woman told me. "It is a complex mixture of love and fear, trust and suspicion. It tends to feed on itself—there is evidence to support any suspicion if one looks long enough and to justify any fear if one broods long enough."

Whether all this is outwardly evidenced by sudden spats, touchiness, and bad temper, or by prolonged and ominous silences, both partners generally know something is very wrong at a time when they most need things to go right. But, most important of all, their ability to communicate, to talk openly and frankly, is curtailed or stopped. So here, too, is another set of dynamics leading to silence and secrecy. This is a consequence that thwarts collaboration and prevents planning and preparation. It puts off the evil hour by pretending it will never arrive.

So all events seem to conspire toward the same outcome: The most difficult kinds of mutual adjustment must be achieved when both partners are least able to collaborate with each other. What seems remarkable to me is that the adjustment is so often made so well. I have wondered whether this means that the crisis is not as severe as I imagine, or even that it is imaginary. But whenever I could get people to talk about their feelings they corroborated some substantial part of my description.

How, then, do couples overcome this crisis? Perhaps in the long years of marriage the partners learn to communicate in very subtle ways, which become substitutes for discussion. They learn to "read" each other sufficiently to be able to arrive at decisions never voiced about problems never openly stated.

Another guess is that the strains generated by imminent retirement radiate to all areas of the relationship and rupture it at its weakest point. This may partially explain the dissolution of long-standing marriages at this stage of life. Although the retirement situation is not often clearly identified among the causes, this may be because it lies so deeply submerged. And sometimes, it would appear, dissolution is the logical way out of an otherwise insoluble dilemma.

An example is that of the couple who started their family early. By the time they were fifty-five, the youngest of their six children was already out of the house at college, and the other five were married or on their own. At this point, the mother was free to reorganize her life and return to her early interest in painting. She soon became a successful portrait painter. However, her husband was fixed in his established routine as a school administrator and committed to a very stressful job that would provide his retirement pension ten years later. Feeling trapped in a demanding job, he greatly resented what he called his wife's "retirement." Her liberation from mothering and housework, her freedom to go off on painting excursions and other holidays, her growing circle of friendships in which he could not or would not participate, exacerbated his feeling of imprisonment in his job. He felt that he was working so that she could enjoy herself.

She saw no reason not to enjoy her freedom, although for some time she pretended to be busy keeping house and putting dinner for two on the table. But for a woman who had raised six children this was a trivial work load. As her own life opened up increasingly, in ways they did not share, she refused to feel guilty about her freedom and was unwilling to bear her husband's increasing resentment of what he considered an unfair relationship. Long before the ten years were up, she struck out on her own and the marriage collapsed.

Buried in the tangle of this shifting relationship was the retirement problem, but only someone looking for it could see it was one of the rocks on which the marriage had foundered.

More often the marital situation is resolved without discussion simply because one partner submits to the other, not fully aware of doing so, not clearly reckoning the price, not entirely conscious of the possibility of any other outcome. This process is often present in many relationships that work for the partners in it. It should also be said that the partner who is dominant, who may be the manipulative one, is sometimes unaware of the role he or she is playing or of the sacrifice the other is being asked to make. Like dance partners, each is responsive to the other and they move in unison, and it is not objectionable to them that one leads, the other follows.

It doesn't always work out—sometimes the resolution is achieved in an opposite way: The marriage breaks up, and one or both find another partner. A man confronting in retirement the task of inventing a new future for himself must think of that future as being a fresh start; a man severed from his roots in his business or profession must learn to think unthinkable thoughts, and among them may be the thought of uprooting his marriage, an idea it may never before have been possible for him to contemplate.

Particularly in a marriage in which the couple has lost all genuine contact and is kept together only by habit and inertia, a man who feels threatened by the need to renegotiate the basic terms of the relationship may find it far easier to begin anew on a clear slate with another woman who is not part of his past. A man who finds it hard or impossible to discuss his fears and concerns with a wife who is being forced into retirement with him may find it far easier to share those concerns with a woman who, though she may be far from retirement age, is ready for a fresh start on a new life with an already retired husband. And, paradoxically, people frequently accept in new partners attitudes and behavior they found intolerable in the old.

Without going into all the factors—sexual, social, financial, psychological—that affect the success or failure of marriages, it is significant to me that these second marriages seem to succeed more often than they fail. This might show that the change was, so to speak, the "correct" one to meet the situation. I find this somewhat surprising, for I have tended to think that to break up a long-standing marriage and enter an entirely new life with a different partner would be pretty risky. My surprise increases when I see the complicated situation that is often created—with both partners to the marriage having living prior spouses, both often having grown children, and both having social networks that have been split by divorce. It becomes hard to tell friend from foe, to repair the rents in the relationships with friends and with grown children. The financial tangle alone is often enough to make lawyers wince and tax accountants blanch. Everything seems to have become far worse. Yet, for the most part, it works out.

My theory is that people have a greater capacity to adjust than we are willing to believe. If I am correct, the question is: Why couldn't the same couples successfully adjust to their retirement problems? Irreconcilable marriage differences are less frequently papered over; divorce and remarriage are rather commonplace these days; and there are plenty of examples and role models to follow. Marital problems and relationships are no longer very secret or private experiences; they are openly discussed and frequently ventilated. There are practitioners (lawyers, social workers, counselors) who give guidance and advice and provide the opportunity to gauge whether one really feels what one says one feels and to discover whether others share these feelings.

Few of these facilities are yet available to potential retirees, who do not have the sense of the commonality of their experience or the validity of their feelings. For the most part, their thoughts and fears are internalized and concealed—often even from themselves. There are few available role models, and practically no effective sources of guidance and advice. If these things are generally true, it would follow that turning the retirement problem into a divorce-remarriage problem is a way of making it easier to solve.

IV. FORCED AND EARLY RETIREMENT

Involuntary retirement has some surprisnig aspects, some of which may be beneficial.

THERE IS AN important distinction between forced and voluntary retirement, as well as between early and "normal" retirement. It must be obvious that the reasons for and the circumstances of retirement play a large part in shaping feelings about it. By "forced" retirement, I mean the instances in which the decision to retire is either made by someone else or dictated by unavoidable circumstances, such as ill health.

In my work, I have often encountered the man who has not only outlived his usefulness to the company, but has also become an impediment. He may have developed health problems that limit his ability to do his work but which he chooses to ignore; he may have developed personality problems expressed in hostility to the company and to his fellow workers, refusal to conform to change, persistent disregard of rules, antagonizing of customers, and general cantankerousness that makes him unmanageable to the people who are his managers. If these characteristics are seen as associated with aging, and if he is within ten years or so of the normal retirement age, the usual solution, instead of firing him, is to negotiate some way for him to retire early. In most cases the employee turns out to have been aware of his unacceptable behavior and to have known on some level that he could not continue. He had been hoping for a way out of the dilemma but could not find the answer by himself. Such a man frequently welcomes an offer of special arrangements for retirement as the best way out of his untenable situation.

Sometimes it is the employee who initiates the idea of early retirement. Generally he has a health problem. Sometimes the reasons are such that, had he been younger, he would simply have given up his job: A crisis in the family requires him to relocate, or he has to devote his time to a personal problem, or he has to conform to someone else's timetable, as in the case of a spouse qualified for retirement.

Where early retirement is a solution rather than a problem, much of its impact is cushioned. It may create other problems, perhaps more numerous but usually less severe. It has a practical and defined reality, however hard it may be to face, quite unlike the arbitrary and artificial boundary line called retirement age.

The so-called mandatory retirement is very much with us. Until recently, it was universally considered to be at sixty-five. It has been pushed back, but it has not been wiped out. The bitterness of a man unwillingly shoved into retirement on the specified birthday is painful to see, but it has an unexpected aspect.

One would assume that a man full of anger and resentment at what he perceives to be a great injustice would have increased difficulty adjusting to retirement, but often just the opposite occurs: The injustice provides a focus for all the unfocused feelings by identifying a target for them. The outrage can be openly expressed, even used to generate sympathy and attention and to relieve tensions and pressures. It reduces the isolation of the individual because he can show and share his anger, and he can openly call for his wife's loyalty and concern in his time of need and trouble. This in no way makes the injury less real or painful, but it does make it more bearable. It even makes his feelings more understandable to others; people who might be blind to the subtleties of retirement can recognize that there is something wrong about a capable man's being forced to stop working before he is ready to stop.

The term "forced retirement" has acquired new inflections recently. One stems from the orchestrated professional effort in the preretirement counseling programs to induce retirement at the time and age that best serve the employer's purposes. If an employee is subjected to a barrage of carefully designed propaganda intended to induce him to take a certain action, can it be said that he has been "forced" to do it? Perhaps not, but it may come to the same thing.

Another comes from the profound consequences of the 1979 legislation generally postponing mandatory retirement to age seventy. It affects an entire generation of employees who had assumed that they would not be permitted to work beyond the age of sixty-five and whose pension plans had been designed actuarially to mature when they reached that age. Now they have been given new options: retiring at sixty-five, as they had expected; opting to continue until seventy; or to retire in any year in between. There are several millions of people who now have choices they have never before had to make, but no obvious basis on which they can make an informed choice. It is far too early to know what the consequences of this dilemma will be, but I think they will be far-reaching.

Finally, there is the more widespread, unrecognized forced retirement I have already mentioned of the wife, who —whether she is working or not—is forced into retirement because her husband retires. He may or may not be "ready for retirement" (whatever that may mean) when he turns sixty-five, but the greater likelihood is that she will be even farther away from "being ready."

One pays a price for entering any life-stage prematurely, for a certain amount of distortion must occur in the relationship when one marriage partner enters a new life-stage that is premature for the partner who must enter it with him.

V. A SENSE OF CLOSURE

A ceremony of retirement is essential but has not yet been invented.

===

THERE IS NO CEREMONY of retirement. The lack is a curious one. There is some sort of celebration rite or ritual to mark all our other major life-stages—birth, marriage, death—as well as their anniversaries, which become events by which we measure the passage of time. Many lesser events are also heralded with some sort of ceremony—school graduations, religious confirmations, and others. But there is not yet a meaningful way to mark the conclusion of one's working life, to celebrate having attained the crucial life-stage of retirement. In contrast to a group experience such as graduation, people retire separately, one by one, and the absence of ceremony to mark their passage makes it even more of an isolating experience.

When an executive retires there is generally some kind of office party, but this does not serve the purpose I have in mind. It is almost identical to the celebration of other events in the company—office parties that celebrate someone's promotion, departure, or the company anniversary. And it generally does not include personal friends or relatives other than wife and perhaps children. All the other people who make up a man's social network are considered irrelevant to this occasion, for it is primarily an event for one's business associates.

Further, there is a spurious geniality about such company occasions. Warm sentiments are publicly expressed by people whose relationship has never been warm or sentimental; words such as "appreciation" and "recognition" and "contribution" are used freely by executives who may not have known the retiree except in the last few years of his career, who could not clearly define what his contributions were, and who are hazy about what they are recognizing and appreciating. As anyone who has attended such functions will agree, they have an air of polite and obligatory showmanship rather than of a shared emotional experience.

This kind of event aside, a man generally reaches the end of his career without the necessary sense of closure. This feeling of completion, of unmistakably having come to the stopping place, is an essential prerequisite to the process of turning away and facing a new direction. Without it, one lingers emotionally at the place from which one should depart. The manner in which a man actually walks out of his office for the last time is very much like the way he has left it so many times before to go on a long vacation or an extended business trip. There should be a way to give this time a very different and significant finality.

What is so different and significant is that the man is not simply leaving the office, the job, and the company. This time he is leaving his lifetime vocation. There is more involved than seeing that his work is left in good order. What a man needs at this point is the sense that his career has also been left in good order, that his working life—all of it, from the first day so many long years ago to the last, spanning all the jobs he has held, all the companies he has served—has now become a completed edifice, a project finished with some degree of satisfaction in the final product.

I don't know how this can be done, but of all the strong

feelings men have expressed to me, the one most consistently present was this: that retirement did not feel like a proper stopping place but more, as one man put it, "like a permanent interruption."

An important element in this need for closure is that at retirement, as I have already mentioned, one relinquishes, all at once, all unattained career goals. This is an act of profound meaning, and it cries out for recognition.

At retirement, executives confront the fact that whatever they have not yet done they will never do; whatever they have not yet won is forever lost; whatever they have not yet changed, improved, or corrected will go on as it is. What they have lost is their potency, their power to affect the future. Without a proper ceremony of closing and renunciation, they have no way to mourn the causes that now become forever unfinished business, to honor the intentions that will never be fulfilled. To turn away from them so casually is to trivialize them and diminish themselves.

VI. SOME ILLUSIONS WE START WITH

The resemblance between retiring and vacationing is deceptive.

MOST PEOPLE SEEM to have similar ideas about what the first day of retirement will be like, and most people are wrong. For example, we all seem to have the same mental image of ignoring our usual wake-up time and turning over to go back to sleep. It's a delicious idea, but almost any retired person will tell you what actually happened that first morning—how very busy he was, getting ready for the movers, getting packed for the trip, getting down to the bank, whatever. I have rarely met a man who really did fulfill that lifelong dream of lounging in bed or who, for that matter, wishes he had.

Busy-ness seems to be the universal remedy for easing the shock of plunging into the unknown.

Another part of the universal dream is "the trip." I have rarely met anyone whose retirement plans did not include some reference to travel. For some people, traveling constitutes the entire program. "The trip" is sometimes setting out in a van or camper on a long tour. (It is always longer than the longest paid vacation one has ever had; the distinction seems to be important.) Sometimes it is a journey in the family car to some never-before-visited destination, sometimes a cruise, a package tour, a trip around the world.

This part of the universal dream, unlike the sleeping-late part, is almost always realized; only a handful of the people I know failed to take the trip on retirement or soon after.

It performs a partially recognized function: It is a reward one gives oneself for a lifetime of work. It is the ultimate vacation.

It performs other functions not so clearly admitted. It is a reassurance, a validation of the fact that all is well, that one's affairs are in order, that one can depart free of care and worry and put anxieties to rest. It is also a corroboration that one is physically fit and active. It serves to verify that one can afford some luxury and is in good financial condition. But most of all, I think, it is a safe first step into the unknown new way of life. One goes to a place never visited before, has a pleasant experience there, and returns safe and well. This is the metaphor of reassurance that one can enter retirement and survive, even enjoy.

But there are two differences that make all the difference in the world between this ultimate vacation and the preceding ones: From this vacation you do not come back and pick up where you left off; you remain retired. And retirement is not for an interval, a measured span of time; it is for as long as you live.

People describing their feelings on returning from "the trip" used such words as "reaction" and "letdown." I often detected some indefinable or indescribable sadness vaguely felt.

A man who, with his wife, toured the Orient to celebrate his retirement, described his feelings on his return. "Every time I'd ever taken a trip or a vacation, I had a sort of reentry experience when I returned—the matter of picking up where I had left off, turning on again all the things I had turned off, the sense of saying, 'Let's see now, where was I?'

"This time, I thought to myself, 'Well, I'm back.' And then I wondered, 'Back to what?' There was nothing to pick up, nothing to resume. I didn't feel I had returned to where I had set out—instead I had arrived at a strange kind of nowhere place, where there was nothing already in motion. I felt a kind of psychological jet lag, as though I were out of phase with everything around me."

There was a strong clue in his analogy—he was saying that some inner rhythm had been disrupted. It seems to me that he was referring to a rhythm most of us have adopted and few are aware of. It goes something like this: When we are young, we go to school until three o'clock and the rest of the day belongs to us. Later we go to work five days a week and the weekends belong to us. We work for someone until we retire and the rest of our life belongs to us.

This rhythm tends to make us think of retirement as though it were a perpetual weekend or a permanent vacation. But the fallacy is that a weekend is a pleasant luxury only because it is an interval between two periods of work. To a person who is unemployed, weekends are very different. What makes the interval precious is its limited duration. When it goes on permanently, leisure time becomes unsatisfying and ultimately loses its capacity to refresh and restore. Finally, in time, like anything carried to excess, it is deteriorating.

This may offer a clue to the phenomenon of death soon after retirement. It may not be the result only of the fact that something vital—career, occupation, or profession—has stopped. It may be partly the result of the subtler fact that retirement, which they entered as though it were an interval, becomes unendurable to some people when they finally realize that it will go on for the rest of their lives.

If this is so, it would seem important to divorce the concept of retirement from its rhythmic but erroneous resemblance to weekends and vacations. The link, however, is being constantly reinforced by those who profit from the leisure industry.

A better way to perceive retirement might be as the beginning of a new stage of life for which we have earned the opportunity for the first time to plan a life-style. There is a younger generation coming along to whom life-style is naturally a matter of conscious choice, but for us who are the first generation of retirees, life-style was something that evolved as the aggregate of innumerable small choices made along the way. We never thought of it as a final product. So this new freedom to make a conscious choice may be harder for us. It calls for an unfamiliar way of thinking, for a certain amount of creative imagination and adventurousness with which it is not now associated.

In this light we might think of retirement as an appropriate time for new directions, long-term purposes, and significant goals, for widening out rather than closing in, for greater diversity rather than a search for security. Retirement could provide the opportunity to overthrow stereotypes and find new rhythms; it could provide a best as well as a last opportunity to give greater meaning to our lives.

We have many advantages over our children, who are so preoccupied finding their identity, asserting their autonomy, and testing their power over their own lives. Unlike them, we can draw on a life wisdom gained throughout our many years, we can act on values we have painstakingly defined, we have a historical view of our own growth and development and the pattern of our lives—and we have learned how to survive. To a great extent we already know ourselves. So for us life can continue to be an adventure because it is no longer an experiment.

VII. DISCOVERIES WE MAKE

Most familiar expectations work out in unexpected ways; a few insights into leisure and voluntarism.

ANOTHER ERRONEOUS VIEW of retirement is that it is an act taken at a single leap. One is working today, retired tomorrow. It doesn't happen that way. Retirement is a process. It is similar to marriage. One may be single today, married tomorrow, but the process of becoming a married person occurs over a period of time. So, too, does the process of becoming a retired person.

I have met very few people who completed this process in less than a year or two; it seems to take that long for retired people to settle into their new roles. In consequence, the first year or two are times of transition, and the transition stage is a time of discovery. One becomes aware of problems not anticipated and of feelings never experienced. One is very much in a state of self-awareness, busy sorting out what is good from what is not, matching actual experience with prior expectation. One tends to watch oneself somewhat critically, somewhat mistrustfully, and constantly to evaluate one's own performance as a retired person.

Most people expect that the major adjustment lies in no longer going to work every day. This generally proves to be surprisingly easy to manage; other changes are harder.

When I asked, "What do you expect to enjoy most when you retire?" the replies—after sleeping late and traveling—almost always included something summarized as "not doing anything I don't want to do" and its opposite, "getting around to doing all the things I've never had the time for." If I pressed for details of the first, I would elicit a little catalogue of petty behaviors, such as no longer having to wear a business suit every day and not having to entertain disliked business associates.

The things one never had time for included spending more time with the family—which frequently proved to be a dubious blessing—and having more time to think, an illusion based on the false impression that thinking is always time-consuming and can never be done simultaneously with anything else. Some were more specific and generally referred to hobbies and skills—writing, making or collecting things, reading, studying, recreation (unlimited amounts of golf, tennis, or sailing), and doing things that take lots of time (building a sailboat or a cabin in the woods). The list sometimes includes research (investigating family roots) or experiment (that mail-order idea) or invention (the well-organized medicine chest).

I am impressed by how many of the things one "never had time for" remain undone or remain forever uncompleted once there *is* all the time in the world. Part of the revelation of retirement is that many of our yearnings are for things we really didn't want, that we have been nourishing ourselves on spurious notions of what we are capable of if only we were not hindered by the need to earn a living, and we discover late in life that we have created our own myths.

Given the time and freedom to write, there may be a plunge into the Great American Novel, but it is usually never completed. We may sign up for a course or two in philosophy or art and then go on to other things, fool around with a few chess books and then lose interest. We may thus actually begin on the great and little adventures we have set such store by, but then find them without nourishment. Part of the adjustment that seems to take place in the early stages of most retirements is this sampling and discarding of long-held ambitions. The result is part of the stripping-down process that is occurring in all other areas of one's inner self, and it compounds the problem of self-identity. One who for decades has answered the question, "If you didn't have to earn your living as a lawyer, what would you be?" by responding, "I would be a novelist, of course," is, when life has granted his wish, forced to acknowledge that he doesn't enjoy writing and perhaps is not very good at it.

The dilemma then becomes, "Now that I am no longer a practicing lawyer and will never be a novelist, what am I? Anything at all?"

A man told me, "I went into retirement with great anticipation, confident that I had a new starting point. I knew exactly what I wanted to do and couldn't wait to get to it. All I needed was the time to spend in the library, doing the research for my book. But five or six months later my enthusiasm had faded. My idea was still a good one; it just didn't grab me anymore, and I knew I would never go through with it.

"Then I began to feel disoriented and helpless at having to find an answer to the question of what I wanted to become. It was a throwback to my childhood when people used to ask me what I wanted to be when I grew up. And it became very important to me that other people not know that I was floundering, that at my age I didn't know the answer to that question. It took me almost two years to get my life into focus again, and most of that time I was pretending to be an active and interested person."

Activity is the operative word at this stage. When work

no longer provides activity, interests and hobbies are substituted. Early in retirement, there is an unnatural carryover of attitudes—men tend to approach their hobbies as they did their work: intensively. The hobby gets the highest priority, the most time, the greatest energy, the extensive investment.

If the hobby is woodworking, he will be able proudly to show you his carpentry shop, complete with every tool and machine he can possibly require, laid out with great ingenuity. He may plan to work on pottery, on gemstones, on taxidermy or oil painting—whatever hobby he chooses will be provided for lavishly, and he will plan to spend long hours pursuing it.

It may be simply a matter of personal bias, but this seems to me to be a perversion of the concept of leisure-time activity; it is not done at all in a leisurely way. It seems more a matter of job replacement than of pleasure, the anxious need to fill an unendurable void.

For many men, this period passes when the adjustment to retirement is finally made. Then the workshop is used for occasional projects, but it is no longer the center of activity.

"I feel a little guilty now when I have occasion to go down to my workshop. When I look over some of the equipment I put in, I know I won't tackle any job big enough to require all that stuff, and that I overreached. I'm still proud of it, and I love to show it to visitors, but I must admit to a little bit of fakery by now because the layout implies much more than I really intend to do."

Another aspect of the plunge into hobbies has to do with what men call "working with your hands." Particularly for men whose only physical effort at work has been carrying an attache case or lifting a telephone, and who spend their days dealing with ideas, tactics, concepts, problems, and other shifting abstractions, there is a yearning to deal with concrete objects, things that can be seen and handled and worked on

74

with tools, problems with physical solutions. Even sports can be seen as a way to provide a touchable, visible, solvable problem, even if it is only the problem of getting the ball into the cup, through the basket, or over the net.

As a relief from the abstract, these things serve the busy executive very well—and they provide something else in the bargain: "All day my head is buzzing—at the office I use my mind every minute, even when I try to relax by looking out the window. By the end of the day I am so revved up that I can't shut it off—I find myself thinking about office matters at dinner, at the theater, even when I wake up in the night. But on the weekend when I get on the lathe and start turning a chair leg in a complicated design, everything else blacks out. I stop thinking about anything but that cutting edge—and it's as though I were resting my mind and giving it a chance to restore itself. After a few hours of that kind of concentration, I feel refreshed." Some men get the same kind of relief just mowing the lawn.

These are familiar ideas, I know, and because they are so familiar we tend to carry them over to retirement, with unfamiliar consequences.

"I wondered why I found rock polishing boring after I retired when it had so interested me before then. You can't let your attention wander when you're grinding a stone it's taken you months to find. When I was employed, polishing demanded enough concentration to keep my mind off other things. But after I stopped working, I had too few other things to think about. What I needed was not something to get my mind off my problems—I needed problems to get my mind working on."

The function of sports and hobbies, then, seems to be opposite in retirement to what it was during employment. In the working years, they served as an antidote, a way of turning off the incessant mental buzzing generated by work, a kind of welcome mindless interval interrupting the constant mental concentration.

But in retirement, the last thing a man seems to need is mindless intervals—he seems to have too little to think about in the first place. He does not need activity that takes his mind *off* things—he needs the kind that puts his mind *on* things.

"What I came to realize is that I consciously had to look for things to think about. Now, that was a startling idea: I never would have believed it if someone had told me it would happen. There never was a time I didn't have things to think about—earning a living, raising a family, managing the household. Even when I first retired, I was busy as hell, and had problems to solve and decisions to make. Once that initial period was over, though, there weren't many new problems coming along, and the decisions were about such things as what I wanted to eat for dinner. I found myself sitting on the porch staring into space, with my mind a blank, although if you asked me I'd say I was enjoying the peace and quiet and looking at the view.

"I began to realize that without having to earn a living, raise a family, manage a household, I'd actually have to find things to think about, that I'd have to provide my own mental input in order to generate any mental output. What an astonishing revelation that was!"

For such purposes, games and hobbies, recreation and leisure-time activities, are inappropriate. One needs interests with meaning, activities that matter, concerns that make a difference in the real world.

Alex Comfort says, "There is marginally more chance of useful social involvement for an older person in a ghetto than for a retired executive . . . who may not recognize that he has been sold a second, non-civic childhood along with the condominium key."

"Useful social involvement" seems essential in making activity meaningful. What springs at once to mind is some kind of volunteer work—in the community, church, hospital, or university. There are well-organized voluntary service organizations, of which RSVP (Retired Senior Volunteer Program) is perhaps the best known, that direct retired people to places where their free services will be used.

It would be unfair to disparage such organizations, the establishments they serve, and the volunteers who work for them. But there is a great deal of cynicism among retired executives about some of the basic assumptions of voluntarism.

Said one man, "The assumption is that once a person has retired, he should be happy to do for nothing what he used to be paid to do. I've always believed that the laborer is worthy of his hire, that you get what you pay for, that nothing good comes cheap, that free advice is worth what you pay for it. So it is very hard for me to believe that people really value my work when I do it for nothing."

"What I most resent," said another, "is being denied the option of forgoing payment. The only condition on which anyone wants me to do anything is that I will do it for nothing."

"The feeling I get," another man said, "is that I have somehow been written out of the economy. I must pay for everything, but no one expects to *pay me* for anything."

The resentment was sometimes spelled out in detail:

"On the one hand, if I'm a patient, the hospital charges me unbelievably high prices, and it charges for every little thing: It has separate charges for the blood and for giving the transfusion, for the use of the equipment and the use of the room, for taking the required blood test and for reading the test, and so on and on. On the other hand, when I'm not a patient, the same hospital would like me to come in and answer the phone, give information, direct visitors, issue passes, distribute books, arrange flowers, collect TV rentals, and do all sorts of other work—but to do it for nothing."

A woman who retired to a college town:

"At the university, professors don't do any research unless they get a grant to do it. One of them, in charge of the archives, spent an hour persuading a group of us retirees to identify old pictures of the campus he had collected. He told us how much satisfaction it would give us. But it was just a way of getting us to do for nothing what he was well paid for."

Another man told me, "The standard attitude is that we retirees are not supposed to earn any money because we get Social Security. That's bunk. We're allowed to earn as much as we please. Above a certain amount, the Social Security is reduced, but that's my own concern, not anyone else's. I can choose to be paid one way rather than another, and I don't want to be denied that choice."

The distinction generally made was that they approved donating time and energy to causes clearly outside commercial considerations, although these did not utilize their best skills: helping build the new church, tending dying patients at a hospice, covering emergency telephones at night for the Rescue Squad, delivering meals for Meals on Wheels. They had no reluctance about aiding people at the outer edges of the business world: guiding youngsters in Junior Achievement, advising the new black enterprise, soliciting work for sheltered workshops and jobs for the handicapped. What they balked at was being used by those with self-interest: the well-paid professor who would take credit for work they did under his direction for the published article that would get him tenure, the doctor who used them in his paid research, the private hospital that saw them as a ready pool of free labor, the "nonprofit" organizations whose paid professionals profited in various ways from their donated services, and anyone who used retired volunteers in ways that deprived working people of jobs. "You sometimes see two people side by side, both doing practically the same work, one a paid employee and the other a volunteer. That tells me it's a con."

It may come down to this: In our culture, value is measured in dollars and expressed in price, so the retired man gets the message that his services have no real value. He is expected to be glad of the opportunity to get the reward of satisfaction rather than the reward of money, because the remaining alternative is the sometimes veiled threat of not being permitted to participate at all.

The guesses and assumptions that people make about what they will dislike about retirement are often wide of the mark, too. When I asked, "What do you expect the bad part to be?" the replies were fairly unimaginative. They included many things that would be missed, such as lunch with the fellows at the office, the commuter-train card game, making important business decisions, and having a secretary. There was mild apprehension about a little too much togetherness during long days at home, about one's friends not being available during working hours, and about possible vague difficulties in "making a good adjustment at first."

One may use both lists—the anticipated pleasures and the bad parts—as a way of estimating how real and clear is the concept of what retirement will be like. Aside from a general conclusion that the prior concepts have very little relationship to the subsequent realities, I found a characteristic that I had not quite expected: The expectations were *trivial*. If one were to use them to formulate a picture of the

79

life-style they imply, what emerges seems to be unfocused and lacking important purpose; there is a faintly childish quality about them that is saddening.

They lack scale and magnitude and mature purpose. They are somewhat shapeless notions that do not seem to justify the effort of having lived so long and gone through so much in order to reach this future. They are evidence, to me, that the prevailing image of retirement has been trivialized, that what could be a rousing act toward the end of the play has been made into a stage wait in the wings, by actors and authors who do not seem able to see the full possibilities of the play.

What limits their vision? I think it is their concept of retirement, to the extent that they have been taught to see retirement as leisure. As Alex Comfort says, "Leisure is a con. It's like saying someone has been recycled by a shark. Leisure should occupy an occasional afternoon, not 20 years. . . . Leisure in our culture means activity which is by definition goalless and irrelevant, and our emphasis on it childrenizes older people."

This view of retirement as *leisure* tends to block out the view of retirement as *freedom*, which is something entirely different.

If we try to examine that difference more closely, our thinking is impeded by the fact that leisure seems to imply freedom, and freedom seems to include leisure—and play seems to involve both. Few of us have the stomach for such semantic exercises, and we do not normally examine such concepts analytically. Thus we become suspectible to accepting, without examining, the widely propagated equation that retirement = freedom = leisure = play.

I do not question that retirement brings freedom—that word turns up in almost every discussion among the newly retired. It is difficult to capture it in words, but the underlying theme as I understand it is a feeling of having been liberated from something one only dimly knew was imprisoning.

"I never really knew how hemmed in I always was until the constraints were lifted," said one person.

"I mostly enjoyed the sense of freedom," another told me, and when I asked, "Freedom from what?" there was a sigh and a pause that told me how hard it was to understand and convey.

Mostly, I think it was what I have come to call *an end to striving*. The more common form is "getting out of the rat race," but that does not say it accurately. What is meant, I think, is that one no longer has to measure up, to achieve, to produce, to deserve whatever is received, to protect and defend whatever one has won. In effect, no one is keeping score anymore; the game is over.

It seems almost logical that a new game should begin, but this time one that is not so deadly serious, one that is fun to play, and without any kind of hazard for the player. Golf and tennis, arts and crafts, fishing and camping, swapping and collecting, all these fit the definition.

But this trail of logic will never lead you to the question that lies at the heart of retirement: "What am I now free *for*?" This is a question that looks to the future, unlike its counterpart, "What am I free *from*?" which looks at the past. The first question produces an entirely different equation: retirement = freedom = release of formerly employed energy = action in new directions.

Contributing to our misdirection is the normal tendency, as we go through the early stages of retirement, to be far more aware of what we have been *freed from* than of any other aspect of our new freedom. Our thoughts, as I shall point out in a moment, revolve far more often about the past than about the future; because we are experiencing so much present change, the future is still blurry. While making the abrupt turn into retirement, we have slowed down for the curve and the road ahead has not yet fully come into view. This is the point at which so many of us go off at a tangent and miss the right road altogether.

"For the first few years the only things I thought worth doing were those that were as opposite as possible to what I had done before. I was determined to enjoy myself in ways I'd never had time for. Now that I'd laid down my responsibilities I was not of a mind to take on new ones. I was free and I intended to stay that way."

Hidden in that statement is the equation: Freedom = leisure. It would be hard to explain to a man from Mars that although children and retired adults have considerable freedom for leisure and play, the resemblance is deceptive. The difference is that the leisure and play of children, unlike those of the retired, are ways of growing and learning, preparation for active and productive lives. In that sense, to say that leisure *childrenizes* older people may be an unintended slur on children.

There is nothing wrong with leisure except as an entire way of life. It is, as Comfort says, appropriate for an occasional afternoon. But mostly it is too trivial a way to use the freedom retirement brings, particularly if we consider how long and hard we have striven to gain it.

Once won, it should bring us pleasure, but successfully retired people discover that their pleasure does not come either from leisure or activity; it arises, rather, from the changed sense of self generated by what they have chosen to do with their freed energies. To illustrate, the retired man who became a mediator in a community dispute settlement center derived his satisfaction not from the activity, which was physically and emotionally draining, but from his new sense of himself as a person helping others equitably resolve almost irreconcilable differences. Such well-chosen activities can provide two elements that cannot be found in leisure or play but are essential for the psychic nourishment of retired people: *identity* and *function*. When his leisure time did not provide the nourishment he needed, the man who had not been "of a mind to take on new responsibilities" formed a local organization that acted as *ombudsman* for patients at a nearby medical center, serving as intermediary between the sick and the administrative staff. Another joined a watch-dog group to guard the rights of the aged residents of local nursing homes. And another helped set up an educational program for the elderly to reduce the dangers of misusing their self-administered medications.

In all such instances, the chosen activity was rooted in personal and social values the retired person had long held but had not earlier had the time and leisure to act out until retirement freed him to do so. One said to me, "What I am doing enables my life to continue to have real meaning—perhaps to become more meaningful." Another spoke of "a sense of personal growth and expanding horizons."

What successfully retired people take most pleasure in, I have concluded, is themselves: who they are and what they are becoming.

VIII. NEW PERSPECTIVES
ON THE PAST

*When we look back we see ourselves in a new light;
how the attitudes we developed at work hamper
us when we retire.*

ONCE OUT OF THE ROLE he had been playing, a man in retirement sees his completed career in a different light. He can see more clearly now, for example, that he always had to subordinate his own objectives to those of his work. This fact had been obscured by his having thought of his work objectives as being his own. Now he can see they really were not.

A marketing man who introduced a new product successfully and gained an impressive share of the market within a planned period would seem to have achieved his objectives. Looking back, however, he realizes clearly what he has only vaguely known: that getting the new product launched was a company objective, not his, and that whenever it collided with his own objectives—spending some time with his children, getting away for a rest, taking a marketing course, reading a novel, improving his tennis, learning chess, or practicing piano—whatever he would have preferred to do was put aside so that he could get on with what he *had* to do. Anything that tended to interfere with earning a living was shunted aside—and earning a living for him was the process of carrying out other people's objectives.

He had always been conscious of being tied to commitments: budget forecasts, production targets, marketing estimates, periodic reports, completion dates, the early-morning planning session, the late-evening dictation session, the informal Wednesday luncheon conference. In retrospect, he realizes how tightly woven was the pattern in which he had been fixed and how little latitude he ever had for the incidental and accidental, the whim or impulse, which were always suppressed or subordinated if they could not fit into the interstices of the net in which he was bound. What he could not see then but can see now is that the net was designed to serve the purposes of the company; it was only in the tiny open spaces that any of his own objectives could be fitted. As a result, they had to be tiny objectives, which tend to be unsatisfying, and often not worth fighting for.

When even these small opportunities are waived, the individual becomes a recognizable workaholic, the person whose work has become his life. Many, but not all, major executives reach this stage. Since the addiction is often without cure, they are forever unable to make any distinction between company objectives and personal ones; they have inextricably merged. The workaholic is the man who phones his associates at all hours of the night, calls them back from their vacations, calls meetings on weekends, and uses holidays for conferences. He becomes the man who hangs on beyond all reckoning and at all costs. If dislodged, he often attempts to continue by replicating his job at another company or forming a company of his own. If that fails, he becomes one of the men whose careers are summarized on the obituary page shortly after retirement.

Most men stop short of this extreme, but most men also go a long way toward it. What we discover in retirement is that we went farther than we thought, and the discovery produces strong reactions.

The principal reaction is quiet indignation that one has sacrificed so much of oneself in the service of others—that is, his wife and children, for whether or not it was actually so, the man can persuade himself that his sacrifices were made in order to provide for them.

These feelings often lead to a flow of egocentricity. I generally hear such phrases as "I'm no longer concerned with goals other people want to set for me," and "Now it's my turn," and "For a change, I come first." We find side by side such contradictions as reducing charitable contributions ("Now that I'm on a fixed income, I've got to think of my own welfare first") and engaging in various kinds of self-indulgence: buying a piano in order to start lessons, joining the health club to stay fit, buying a new wardrobe to replace the business suits no longer worn every day, buying an outboard motor because rented ones are unreliable. No matter what the ostensible reason, this is the giving of gifts to oneself as compensation for all the things that (one has now discovered) one gave up in the past.

These are more or less overt behaviors very strongly related to the way a man sees himself, in retrospect, as having made sacrifices in order to provide for others.

"It was not the getting up and going to work every day, the long hours, the frustrations, the weekend-filling briefcase, the strains and tensions that were the price I paid." The speaker was a recently retired director of creative merchandising for a toiletries manufacturer. "The real price," he continued, "was in the time my work took me away from my family—all the summers they stayed on at the beach while I went back to the city, the trips, the outings, the occasions they enjoyed without me, the fact that I saw so little of my children when they were growing up that I never really got to know them well, that I had so little leisure time to spend with my wife, that I sat at dinner with my mind on business problems while everyone else was talking about what had happened during the day while I was at work. The real sacrifice was in not being able to share their lives, which were lived independently of me a good deal of the time."

But not all men feel this kind of loss, or perhaps do not attach great importance to what this man so regretted losing. They feel rather that they have had to put up with a great deal of hassling from their families, of interference and distraction, which made pursuing a career much more difficult. Some feel they succeeded in their work despite, not because of, their wives and children, who never realized or made allowance for the tough row they had to hoe day after day.

When the truth is told, many men do not really work only to make a living for themselves and their families; their primary motivation always was or ultimately became a quest for success, for victory.

A divorced woman, speaking of her former husband, said, "Bob was always so wrapped up in his work that I often wondered why he had gotten married and started a family. We were divorced soon after he retired, and when the shock subsided and I was able to sort things out more clearly I recognized the pattern—Bob was like a mountain climber, scaling the peaks of success. That was what mattered to him most: getting to the top. And he did manage to get quite high. He needed us for exactly the same reasons a mountaineer needs a base camp—we took care of all his primary needs, arranged everything necessary to get him off to a good start, and we kept moving up behind him so he always had a secure place to come back to before he set out again.

"It wasn't a matter of his providing for us, no matter what he claimed. The fact was that we were providing for him. The proof was that when he was finished climbing—when he got as far as he could go, and retired—he no longer needed us. The expedition was over. The divorce was like breaking camp—folding the tents and going our separate ways."

What seems significant is that regardless of what motivates men to work—whether for their families' sake or their own or some mixture of the two—it is the work that must generally come first, and the family that consequently comes second. Whatever time and attention he has given to his work, for whatever motive, the time and the attention were withheld from his home and family. This is not as insensitive as it may sound; it is often the product of a clear understanding and a willing collaboration between a man and his family. The standing rule in many households is that the provider must be allowed to fulfill his obligations to his family by first fulfilling his obligations to his employer; the job comes first because all else depends on it.

If this is the man's family role—that he is the provider, the breadwinner—the long-term consequences add immeasurably to the difficulty of his becoming a full-time member when he steps out of it.

We do not often think of these long-term consequences, or of the fact that the man who sees his primary family role as the provider must find a way to live within a paradox: that to serve his loved ones best, he must serve his employer first. The better he wants to provide for his family, the more he must turn away from them. There are innumerable ways people perform this kind of emotional acrobatics, which exact a great price.

Most men think and speak in terms of compartments when they refer to the problem at all. "I keep my family in one compartment and my job in another and try not to mix them up" is a typical explanation. "When I go home, I put my job out of my head; when I go to work I put family matters aside" is another. This is a practice of fractionating the personality, another way of living only partially at any one time. It calls for sorting out and separating internal experiences, closing and opening inner doors, suppressing the inappropriate, stunting and editing spontaneous emotions. This is a form of self-control that divides the personality. It is not too difficult to learn, because one has to learn it anyway in order to survive in the business world: One learns to control (that is, to repress or falsify or invent or magnify) one's feelings and opinions so as to make them appropriate to the strategy of the business situation.

The process of distortion goes on in the home at the same time, for if the job is to get first priority, then the job holder must be shielded from home and family crises. Unless they become too severe (that is, out of control), they must be damped down and somehow contained before they reach the proportions at which they may endanger the man's ability to hold his job or perform it properly. ("Don't bother Dad about the car; he's got a report to do for the office.") This dictates the way family problems are addressed and solved—indeed, it identifies whose problems they are or are not. Minor crises tend to be solved without him, and the major ones in which he does participate are generally resolved by summary and abrupt actions and decisions so as not to prolong them, to get them out of the way as quickly as possible. The process holds his participation to a minimum, while respecting his right to intervene at a certain order of magnitude. When he does, his participation carries a hidden message that calls for expedient and conclusive action and tends toward what executives like to call "decision making."

But in the business world, decision making is based on criteria that are inappropriate to family life. Learning to make business decisions that produce optimum results in the most efficient way creates the habit of seeing the much more personal family problems similarly, to regard human problems in business terms, to deal with them efficiently rather than lovingly, to use manipulation and diplomatic guile in situations calling for empathy and caring, to focus on the problem rather than the people, and to think in terms of "results."

This carryover produces such phenomena as the "democratic" family conference—the counterpart of the business meeting—with its careful concern for procedure, voting rights, and agenda, but where spontaneous expressions of human emotion can be and often are ruled out of order. It also produces the managerial father, who hears the facts (gets the reports) and gives or withholds approval (okays or turns down) of proposals, suggestions, requests (recommendations). He is the parent who schedules the time he will be free to discuss what his children want to talk to him about and "gives" them what he considers to be generous amounts of his time. He is the objective one who, although concerned with family harmony, is somewhat above and outside of most of its concerns. He is frequently in the role of the nonplaying coach, helping the team to win but always from the sidelines, never on the field.

Wives and children tune in to this style of behavior quickly and early and often find it reasonable, workable, and acceptable—sometimes because they do not know of a better way. I do not want to pass judgment on this way of life but rather to point out that it exacts a special price when the husband retires. When he steps down from his privileged elevation and leaves the world of business, he cannot simply step into the family scene as though he had been away for a little while. He actually has never inhabited it as a full-time member before, and when he tries to find his place he is like an abdicated king trying to become an ordinary subject of his former kingdom. He is limited by what he was, as well as by what he has become, by how the others have learned to see him and how they have learned to relate to him. It is not a problem of reentry—it is a problem of arrival, not only a problem for himself but for his wife and family as well.

No matter how he goes about it, this process of finding a comfortable full-time place for himself must disrupt the lives of those who share the same environment. As one woman told me, "It is like having your husband crawl into bed after you have long since gotten comfortably settled down. All at once there is a pushing and a shoving, a tugging at the blankets, such turnings and poundings on the pillow, that you can never get back into the original position that felt so good."

A man who has been ambitiously competitive and who has learned to sacrifice others for his purpose when necessary in his work is capable of overriding a son, a daughter, or a wife to achieve ends he considers desirable. He rarely defines it in this way: he has learned to keep an eye on results, on "the bottom line," and to push out of the way anyone or anything standing in his path. This is the way "successful" people in business learn to push for results, to force events. When such a man returns to his home life, he brings some of his arsenal with him—the weapons that have served him well and that gave him his ability to win.

He continues to be autocratic; he will not be pushed or shoved; he sees everyone around him as either an ally or an opponent; he thinks in strategies rather than concerns; he has enormous confidence in his own judgment, and is not easily deflected from his chosen targets by the feelings or reactions of others. He brushes aside sentimental notions and emotional outbursts, is contemptuous of "feminine" logic (his wife) and inexperience (his children). He is a "take-charge guy," who tackles his retirement like a project and sees his family as the staff assigned to help him complete it.

He sets about making "order" in a household in which he has always tolerated a certain amount of disorder because he had more important things to do. He has become blunted to the realization that human relationships are never "orderly," nor are they logical, nor are they efficient, nor can they be organized. Even if he knows this in an intellectual way he cannot respond to it on an emotional level; the necessary flexibility, tolerance, trust, concern for others are all stunted and undeveloped capacities, because they have been so long repressed and so little exercised.

Lacking the ability to alter his way of relating to others, and of relating to his wife and family particularly, he attempts simply to transfer his base of operations from his office to his home, where his arrival is felt as some sort of natural disaster. If there are children remaining in the household, they will be the first to scatter. Sometimes his wife will be able to flee at least some of the time. Often his retirement is coincident with her starting to go to work, for various expressed reasons but primarily to get out of spending so much time in the same house with him.

"The rule in our house had always been not to meddle in Dad's business affairs. We were taught not to touch his papers, not to interrupt his meetings, not to distract him with questions, not to talk with anyone else about what we overheard, to keep quiet when he was on the telephone, not to call him at the office unless it was really important, and not to take too much of his time.

"All of a sudden, it was all turned upside down. Now he wanted to tell us about what he did; he expected us to help him find things he mislaid, criticized us for not taking an interest in what he was doing. He wanted me to know how his filing system worked, where he kept his paid bills, to remind him of his appointments, keep an eye on his calendar, and give him our attention a good deal of the time. It was not exactly like being a secretary, but it wasn't like being a member of the family either."

One of the surprises I encountered was the man who had never developed a true relationship with his wife during all the years he was career building; because there was practically nothing to restore, it proved possible for them to make a fresh start. Many people have difficulty in getting back to "where we were" and in "getting to know each other all over again," but some men who have never known their wives in the first place, and who have no sentimental regard for the earlier relationship, are able simply to set off in a new direction and develop a completely new relationship with her as though they were strangers. For that is what they were.

IX. FREE TO BE YOURSELF

*How it feels to come out from behind the personality
you developed in your working life.*

LOOKING BACK ON his now completed career, every retired
executive realizes that he had always been under considerable
surveillance. That is not quite the way he thought of it in the
past; he generally was not really aware of it; it was an unex-
amined part of his way of life, a pressure so constant that he
long ago stopped sensing it.

It derives from the fact that no one's status in the business
world is guaranteed and permanent; it is always dependent on
someone or something else. It is affected by events and by
what other people think of us—our subordinates, our peers,
our superiors, and our adversaries. There is always someone
whose good opinion of us is essential, someone to whom we
are in some way accountable, who can help or thwart us, ac-
celerate or impede our progress. This is true no matter how
high one rises. Even presidents and board chairmen serve at
the pleasure of others and can, like kings, be deposed. No
matter how powerful the allies one may have in high places, it
takes only a heart attack, a resignation, a reorganization, to
wipe out this resource. So one does not get very far in the
business world without learning the importance of cultivating
the good opinion of others.

This means constantly assessing what others will think if one does or fails to do this or that, down to the pettiest details. If the client or supervisor is a golfer, one speaks to him in golfing jargon; if the boss tends to dress formally, the staff tends to wear conservative clothes. Whatever attribute is highly valued by the Other—punctuality, perhaps, or brevity —is adopted in one's own behavior. One soons learns to meet the expectations of others if the others are "important." In the process, we assume and believe that the Other responds, consciously or not, to the things we are doing and knows, at some level of awareness, what we do and how we act.

We constantly work at creating our most acceptable *persona* for those around us, and it would be hard to say how "real" it is. Certainly it seems authentic to us. It is this *persona* that is under constant surveillance by us and by those around us. We immerse ourselves completely in the part we are playing and avoid doing anything that would be out of character. We have lunch at places that are in keeping with our role and even calculate the size of our tips to accord with it. We consider whether it would be wise to be seen going into an X-rated movie, what impression would be made by the contents of our attache case if we opened it in the view of others, whether the way we answer the telephone produces the desired image. We study the effect on others of the pictures we choose for our office walls, how the size of the desk and chair conforms to our own visual dimensions, even how others evaluate our choice of secretaries and what rewards or penalties are involved in dissenting so often from the consensus at staff meetings.

In time, this behavior tends to become the background against which we display ourselves, a running commentary of unending judgments made by others to which we give heed and which influence us almost automatically, like a continual monitoring signal. We are aware of it, but we never fully realize how completely attuned to it we have been until, on retirement, the signal conveys a strange new message.

It begins to dawn on us that we are no longer subject to the judgments of others. There are no longer any risks in the way we dress, the opinions we express, the way we act, and the things we do. We can come out from behind our *persona* and show ourselves as we really are. We have been disguised so long, however, that we emerge as strangers to ourselves, like a bearded man who finally sees himself clean-shaven again.

It probably still matters whether or not people like us, but their approval, or lack of it, has no practical effect on the progress of our career, our earning power, our influence in the business world. So we can disregard their disapproval if we wish, with impunity.

This release extends in all directions. We can allow ourselves to be seen reading trashy novels and can stop serving Perrier water, we can be careless about our choice of neckties (or stop wearing them), we can stop carrying a pen and pencil in an inside pocket, and can admit unashamedly to having nothing to do. We can do all sorts of things badly and clumsily, express opinions that run counter to what everyone else is thinking, ignore styles and fashions, admit to not knowing things we might be expected to know and not understanding things we might be expected to understand. More, we can expose our complete lack of interest in them—all with impunity.

"Jones always said my greatest fault was to shoot from the hip, to make snap judgments. He was wrong, but I always had to take his opinion into account in calculating my own reaction behavior: Was I validating his impression, or dispelling it? I automatically behaved responsively to his judgment of me. Now it no longer matters whether he was right or wrong, because it no longer matters whether or not I make snap judgments. I can make all the snap judgments I please."

This is a special and unexpected kind of freedom that gives

considerable pleasure in the early stages of retirement—at least until Jones has faded into the past and we have stopped thinking about him altogether.

But we do think about Jones quite a bit in these early stages; we carry on a protracted silent dialogue with him inside our heads. We still feel the momentum of our awareness of what he and others think of us, and we express our new freedom by repositioning our relationships unilaterally in almost everything we do.

One man I know, whose boss had always been a martinet about his staying slender and keeping fit, enjoyed the gooiest of desserts every evening, and he always accompanied the first delectable spoonful with a mental "Up yours, George!" Another had long mental conversations with his associates, urging them not to devote the rest of their working lives to this unworthy company that didn't really appreciate them. And another enjoyed fantasies of making an impassioned plea to the Board of Directors to improve their pension plan—and of their inviting him back to head up the project.

These are in the nature of mental static, echoes from the past, like the noises a machine makes as it slows to a halt after the power has been turned off. In time the static subsides.

The process of restoration, of re-placing oneself at the epicenter of one's universe, often has a displacing effect on one's wife and family, who begin to feel intruded upon by the more insistent presence. This feeling is reinforced by the freed-up attitude of "It's my turn" and "I come first." Family tensions that may have been finely balanced get off center; people who feel they are being shoved have a tendency to shove back. For many families at this stage, as constraints and inhibitions are lifted, it becomes friction time.

Characteristic behavior at this stage includes a tendency to dogmatism (statements beginning with, "I don't care what anyone says . . .") and to assertions that this is how things are and how they will be, rather than, "What do you think?" This tyrannical behavior seems to stem from a compelling need for some show of power and influence in the home, perhaps to compensate for their loss in the business world. The situation is likely to provoke a wife to say, "You can't just give orders around here. I'm not your secretary. Stop bossing me around."

This stage of retirement often involves much pushing-shoving, displays of selfishness, petty bickering, and arbitrary behavior as well as a heightened sensitivity to insult or injustice and greater difficulty in making peace after a quarrel. One hears more frequently such classic accusations as "I don't understand you," "I don't know what you want from me," "There's no pleasing you, no matter what I do," "The older you get, the harder you are to live with," and "What's gotten into you?"

Signals pass back and forth, and covert messages mixed with subtle threats, warnings, and putdowns. There is a constant testing of wills and long silences that say, "I can be as stubborn as you."

The wife feels threatened and invaded, the husband rootless and displaced, and the essential stability of the marital relationship is being tested. It is like a suspension bridge in a high wind. The structure is either inherently stable enough to withstand the stress of increased flex and oscillation, or it collapses. Given his or her state of mind and situation, there is almost nothing either partner can do at this point to *strengthen* the relationship; it is all one can do merely to sustain it.

This pushing-shoving is the process of revising the rules. On some deeper level, it is the process of bargaining and negotiating. Both people are saying, "Things are going to have to be different around here from now on," and each is attempting to shape the new arrangement. They are relocating the boundaries where husband and wife begin to intrude into each other's private space, and altering the precarious balance between solitude and loneliness, between privacy and isolation.

The various ways in which men and women share their lives with each other are unlimited; so there is no end to the variety of scripts by which the same basic plot can be acted out.

As other actors appear in the family drama, the complications multiply enormously; the presence of an unmarried son or daughter may bring it to levels worthy of a Greek playwright. I do not feel qualified to speak with anything more than conventional wisdom about the interplay among a husband at an early stage of retirement, a wife, and a son or daughter asserting adulthood. It is a classic triangle that involves many forces, including the passing of power from one generation to the next, the passage from dependence to independence to domination, the waxing and waning of sexual prowess, the ingratitude of children, and the resentments of elders.

X. OUR GROWN-UP CHILDREN

No matter how adult they are, our retirement profoundly affects them.

THE RETIREMENT OF parents is rarely, if ever, thought of as being an event in the lives of their children, but it seems actually to be a major event. This is perhaps one of the most unexpected discoveries about retirement. Sometimes the discovery is made much later, when a son or daughter feels able to speak of it openly; sometimes it is never made known; and sometimes it is evidenced in such apparently unrelated behavior that the true cause of that behavior is concealed.

It is probably not the simple fact of retirement that precipitates these strong reactions in sons and daughters, but retirement accompanied by relocation and the consequent building of a new way of life. Perhaps the act of "moving away" is the cause, and the fact of retirement merely the accompaniment. Regardless of the cause, although these reactions seem almost universal, they are almost never discussed and rarely written about.

An exception is an article in *The New York Times* by Randi Kreiss. "My parents have retired to Florida, and I am suffering an empty nest syndrome. They taught me the value of family, urged me to settle in town, nurtured the love of my children, and then they left. I may be 31 years old and a liberated woman, but it still hurts. There are thousands of people like me, experiencing a kind of delayed separation anxiety. Our parents are leaving the old hometown and shaking our roots loose as they go. . . .

"Part of me is happy for them. . . . [T]hey have made a gutsy move. Methodically, they lightened their load, sold their house and my father's dental practice, and bought an apartment in Florida.

"But somewhere inside, I'm uneasy. Certainly my own life, my husband's life and my children's lives are diminished by their absence. . . . [T]he balance . . . is missing, the balance between past and present, and the balance between my identity as a child and as a mother. . . .

"Perhaps this is self-centered—I may be unwilling to see my parents retire because it is another confirmation that I too am getting older.

"There is anger in me as well. The child inside is holding her breath and turning blue. . . ."

After describing how the members of the family all clustered in the same neighborhood, she goes on, "So there we were, all settled in, reveling in our togetherness, except Mom and Dad, apparently. They smiled lovingly at us and announced their impending retirement.

"I'm the first one to admit it was childlike but I was angry. My father was always quoting Margaret Mead on the value of an extended family. Now he wanted to deprive his grandchildren of that experience.

"Once the decision was made, my parents began shedding possessions as a dog shakes out fleas. For my husband and me, that house was part of our youth and our romance. Memories mixed with the dust and plaster as pictures came down and relics were hauled up from the basement. . . .

"Maybe part of the sadness was the air of finality. There were unmentioned but strongly felt parallels to the cleaning out and closing up that accompanies a death. My parents vacuumed up every trace of themselves, and left town."

Among the notable things in this unusually frank account is that the daughter concealed her strong feelings of anger, betrayal, and loss. But she does not seem to think that her parents may have concealed their feelings also; she assumes that their feelings about such major life changes as selling their home and everything in it, and retiring from the dental practice, the community, and the family circle were far less profound and upsetting than her own. I greatly doubt this. I can believe that the parents, so profoundly preoccupied with their own hidden feelings and secret thoughts, were not aware of the fact that they were shaking loose their daughter's roots or even that she was angry with them, because she hid her feelings and concealed her thoughts from them.

This is typical of what I have called the conspiracy of silence—the retirement experience seems to isolate each affected person within a prison of secret feelings. But common sense tells me that a family undergoing so strong an emotional experience must evidence it in some way in daily behavior, and I would guess that expressions of these feelings surfaced in ways that very carefully concealed their cause, their nature, and their intensity, that the tensions were expressed as differences of opinion and disagreements about comparatively "safe" matters, such as how to dispose of the contents of the house.

In this account, the parents and the child apparently continued to act out "acceptable" roles, knowing no other way of dealing with their strong and unexpected feelings and having no precedent or model to show them how to do it better or differently.

Certainly, the parents, seen here as going off hand in hand on a carefree jaunt toward a Florida sunset, were acting out the retirement stereotype, possibly because they did not know there was any other, or possibly because the daughter does not know of any other way to think of people who go into retirement. This is the way the conspiracy of silence works.

In two major respects, the daughter's account echoes feelings I have already mentioned: the parallel of retirement with death and dying and the unwanted onset of what Simone de Beauvoir calls the Coming of Age. The account hangs heavy with the threat of impending endings, the sadness of time running out, although this time the feelings are those of the daughter, not of the parents.

If we assume, as I think we can, that the parents and the child had similar feelings, this should have made it easier for them to be open with each other. But neither generation seemed to know that the other was feeling the same things; so each felt compelled to play the expected role: the carefree parents, the approving child, each deceiving the other and thus requiring the other to respond "appropriately" to the deception.

Another example of the generally unsuspected impact of retirement and relocation on grown children, this time involving my own family: As Randi Kreiss' parents did, my wife and I sold our home, disposed of our possessions, and set out on the road to a new life, but we did not settle down for almost a year. During that time we traveled, exploring alternative communities, and unless we made a telephone call, could be reached only by mail sent to our lawyer's office for forwarding.

Some months later, while we were on the road, our daughter suddenly left college at the end of her junior year, moved in with relatives on the other side of the country and took a job, gave it up and moved to another city, rented an apartment there and got a job, and before she started work gave up both the apartment and the job and reenrolled in college a week after the new term had begun. At each step she gave us plausible and acceptable reasons for her decisions, and never did any of those reasons have anything to do with us.

Meanwhile, our son, who was overseas in military service, stopped writing altogether. We did not hear from him for more than six months and could not fathom what could have alienated him so deeply.

After nine months of searching, we decided on a place to live and began to establish our new life. The week we moved into our new home was the week our daughter went back to college. When we sent him our new address, our son began to write us again. It was only then that we began to see the link between our uprootedness and their disconnection.

Although our children may see it differently, my wife and I now believe that when we uprooted ourselves, we "shook their roots loose," too. Neither child had lived at home for some years, and, like Randi Kreiss, both had seemed to approve what we were doing, although we all acknowledged the change would call for some adjusting.

It was a wrench for us to sell our home; we had never considered it to be a piece of real estate or an investment— for us it was the place where we had raised our children, planted trees, and where every room held memories. But none of us realized that to our son and daughter "home" was also a feeling, a symbol. For them, "home" was the place where parents remained and children departed.

We had assured them that we were "still a family," that wherever we were we would always provide a place for them, and that they were always welcome to join us.

But we did not know the extent to which the place where we had lived or, more abstractly, the fact that there was a specific, familiar place where their parents were, was for our children a fixed point, firm ground in a shifting world. It was a place from which they measured psychological distance; it was what they were growing away from, achieving independence of.

It was, we came to believe, essential for children to have such a point of departure in order to achieve adulthood and independence. Someone said, "There are two lasting things we can give our children. One is wings, and the other is roots." Neither seems possible without the sense of place that tells them where "home" is.

It is too late to ask ourselves whether we should have allowed ourselves to become a "homeless" family, however temporarily, even though we made all sorts of practical arrangements to maintain family ties. The important point is that all of us could have managed the painful transition so much better if we had realized more fully what we were doing, had anticipated and better understood the emotional consequences, and had dealt with them openly, rather than permitted each family member to endure a difficult experience privately and separately.

Among the less familiar and more surprising forces that retirement sets in motion, its effects on family members are perhaps the most deeply concealed and least understood. They add immeasurably to the complications of the retirement process because they are too rarely foreseen, too often misinterpreted, and too infrequently taken into account.

So, particularly in the nuclear family, retirement involves more than the uprooting of the man who retires; it can severely strain, or even topple, the structure of the family.

XI. SHIFTING FAMILY
RELATIONSHIPS

*In a family, everyone's role changes when the
principal provider retires.*

THE FAMILY IS affected in other ways. Where the man retiring
has had a position of some authority, it has by reflection given
status to everyone related to him. A wife's social position is
affected, if not determined, by her husband's level of prestige
in his work. If she does not have her own career, it is often
the primary way she is identified among her peers. We frequently hear it in the way she is introduced to others—by her
name, but her husband's credentials: "Mary Jones, Professor
Jones' wife." This extends to older children also; the college
student soon knows which of his peers have prestigious fathers
and which do not.

To whatever extent this plays a part in the lives of family
members—and it may be of no great importance to some—
when the principal provider loses the role that gave him status,
the rest of the family also loses that status. Mrs. Conway,
wife of the vice-president of a large corporation, becomes Mrs.
Conway, whose husband is retired. Tom Conway no longer
says his dad is in charge of production at Amplex. "What
does your father do, Tom?" "Nothing. He's retired."

This is not necessarily felt or seen as a comedown, or

expressed as a grievance. But at some level a person cannot help being aware of and affected by any change in the way he is perceived and identified by others. My point is that the person who retires is not the only one who is de-roled.

There is loss of another role involved with status and identity: the provider's role. Logically, a man who has arranged his affairs so that he can retire on a continuing income from pension, Social Security, and investments is still a provider. But feelings have little to do with logic. Many people are unable to shake off the definition of the breadwinner as *the person who goes to work*. They do not see as a provider a person whose income has little or no apparent connection with working. Jones is not perceived as a breadwinner when his money arrives automatically from the pension fund, from the bank, or from the government even if Jones is doing no work at all.

If Jones has the same idea of what a provider is, he feels himself no longer to be one. The act of providing, while arranged for by him and earned by him, seems to have been delegated to others. His role is more ambiguous and less admirable; there is an irrational suggestion of goofing off, of freeloading, in the way others may see Jones, and a faint whiff of guilt in the way he sees himself. Now that his income is no longer directly related to his efforts, skills, or abilities, he is no longer the active provider.

There is nothing in the work ethic that gives value to the retired provider, although one generally becomes a retired provider only by diligence and prudence over a lifetime. Jones retains his clout as the person in charge of the family economy and the one who controls the money, but his right to that authority has become clouded. The fact is, the family economy no longer depends on him. *If he has arranged his affairs properly, it will get along just as well without him.* He knows this and thus feels less needed by the family at the time he knows he is apparently not needed at all by his former employer. It is one more assault on his self-esteem, one more step in the process of diminishment.

Paul Tournier has written, "What we must do is put an end to the way that we all discriminate between those people who work and those who do not work, between those whom we value because of their work and the others, whom we disparage; it is a form of discrimination which we make even in our own lives between the time we spend at work, looked upon as important, and the time we spend in leisure pursuits, which we consider to be valueless." It calls for the profound recognition, as Henri Nouwen points out, that our worth is not the same as our usefulness.

XII. LOST SATISFACTIONS

The achievements, distractions, and anxieties of the job prove to have been forms of psychological nourishment.

ANOTHER SUBTLE PHASE in this changeover stage of retirement has to do with achievement as a form of psychological nourishment. Everyone enacting his role in the business world does some things that entitle him to at least a momentary sense of satisfaction. There is a steady flow of low-key achievement and reward, aside from the high points of special accomplishments and the low points of frustrations and reverses. We are inclined to pay much more attention to the highs and lows than to the daily flow, which seems routine. So we are often unaware that we have been on a steady diet of small satisfactions, and we do not know we have become addicted until the supply stops.

A man goes through his business day scarcely noticing the little upbeats he felt when he made his point effectively at the morning planning meeting, when he found a way to have a private talk afterward with the plant manager and tighten up their loose relationship, and when he completed the Brimmer project right on target that afternoon, got to the bottom of his dictation folder, and, before he left for the day, read the draft of his monthly report and knew it was good.

Most men seem to require this form of nourishment, although the maintenance level may vary from one person to another. Because the working situation tends to provide it, most men seem unaware that it has become necessary to them.

But retirement does not work that way—it does not assure a flow of accomplishment and satisfactions. In the early stages, there does not seem to be any way in which they can be provided. There is no continuous level of activity that throws off these small sparks of satisfaction; the early stages seem instead to be a period of discontinuity, of stops and starts, of isolated and one-time problems. The peaks and valleys, the highs and lows may be there, but the small emotional gratifications of the "ordinary" day are absent. In the early stages of retirement no day is ordinary, and nothing has yet become routine.

The same subtle sense of something lost or missing can be found in the opposite: One also misses the rather constant weight of pressure and distraction. It is something like the feeling the hiker gets when he takes off his backpack at the end of the day. His muscles flex differently, his sense of balance is altered, and his center of gravity has shifted.

That is what happens early in retirement when the pressures of meeting commitments, keeping to schedules, following plans, fulfilling obligations, keeping pace with events, and dealing with all the other forces that determine our velocity throughout the day are turned off.

We go on for a while with a certain amount of inertial momentum, but very soon we begin to have a strange feeling that unless we push ourselves, we don't go. Only then do we understand that the pressure of responsibility was an energizing force. We must now learn to function without it.

Distractions, too, although we always found them unwelcome, seem in retrospect to have had practical value. The phone call that interrupted dictation of the crucial paragraph of our report, the need to listen to Joe's complaint just before the meeting started (when we wanted to use that moment mentally to prepare a good opening statement), the arrival of the visiting vice-president at the planning meeting when we were halfway through our proposal, all these off-putting interruptions were deplored at the time. In retrospect, we realize they were also stimulators, helping us maintain a high level of alertness, quickening response time, keeping supple the capacity to adapt to a changing situation, although at the time they happened all we were aware of was our dismay.

In retirement there is no larger structure into which we must fit, our schedule does not intersect with others at every point, there is no catalogue of commitments, timetables, and objectives that constitute a tight-knit framework calling for great dexterity in the use of time and attention. Instead, nothing really has to be done now if we prefer to do it later, and practically no one is affected by whether or not it is done at all. Pressure must be almost entirely self-generated rather than imposed by others and by outside events. Interruptions and distractions have an entirely different character. They are far less provocative and disturbing. So they are far less stimulating.

Thus, you become aware that some vital fluid has stopped flowing. The perceptive eventually identify it as the adrenalin that was generated by the pressures and tensions of work as well as the satisfactions. When these stopped, the flow diminished to a trickle. It is almost always expressed in specific terms: "I miss the excitement of getting the spring line together," or "I used to get a kick out of planning a new product introduction." What you now call the "kick" or the "excitement" was then felt as intensified pressure, interrupted by distractions, that left you exhausted at day's end, wondering how much longer you could go on that way.

At some level of awareness, the new retiree realizes that

a source of his vitality has been cut off and that he must exert himself to avoid falling into a deadly lassitude. I know very few men who have admitted to this apprehension, maybe because to do so would be to admit a possibility that might become real if it were put into words. Most men laugh at the idea and speak of being "busier than ever." And most men are very concerned with the level of their busy-ness, go to extraordinary lengths to make busy work for themselves, and thus reveal a great anxiety about it.

Extreme anxiety can be paralyzing, but, like pressure, anxiety can also be an energizing force. It is easily generated, and if you look back carefully, you can see that it served a constructive purpose in your career and can now be used in a slightly altered form to serve the same purpose in retirement. Its function is to enable you to mobilize, to call on your strengths and rally your defenses. When the stimulation provided by pressure, satisfaction, and distraction is no longer present, that provided by anxiety makes a functional substitute to prevent lapsing into lassitude and inertia.

It is almost as if we sense that, for many of us, struggle is essential to survival—and that there must be something to struggle against. The capacity to struggle must be fueled by inner forces when outer forces no longer provoke the adrenalin flow. In that sense we are all addicts who must get our kick, one way or another; the alternative is too awful to contemplate. What we are struggling against is not placidity but paralysis, the leveling down to a monotone, the loss of sharp reflex. Our great dread is that the jiggling marker will steadily subside until it draws a straight line, like an electrocardiograph of a lifeless thing.

XIII. LET'S HAVE LUNCH

Practically no one expects the loss of lunchtime to
be felt so severely.

THERE ARE OTHER ASPECTS of our working lives that we did
not know were important to us until they ended. One that is
immediately recognizable and almost never anticipated is the
loss of the lunch period.

Lunchtime in the business world is far more than a time
to eat—it is the period of interaction, for the development
and testing of relationships, for transacting the interpersonal
business of the day. It is the time for reaching out, smoothing
over, and negotiating, for bestowing favor, showing respect,
sounding out; it establishes status, fixes the pecking order,
and serves as a form of political courtship. It is a meaningful
ritual and often an elaborate one. Who extends the invitation,
who is the host and who the guest, who decides the place, and
what one orders, how they meet and who else is present, how
long one remains and the order of the departure, these are
forms of communication widely understood although as in-
tricate as the subtleties of international diplomacy.

To some men of the business world, the luncheon meeting
is the most important part of the day. In the executive dining
rooms of large corporations it is a significant extension of the
workday. To the newcomer, it is a test and an ordeal. To the

veteran, it is a way to hold court. To the striver it is an opportunity, to the loser an embarrassment, to the harried a reprieve, and to the overworked a restorative. Whatever its function, I think it undeniable that it is important; yet we do not fully anticipate that its absence in retirement will be significant. It is.

In retirement, a man generally has lunch at home. This at once takes it out of the class of both social and business occasions. There is usually no one else, except his wife, with whom he eats at midday. The purpose of lunch at home is to eat—perhaps the least important aim of the business lunch —and all the other aspects of the lunch period are absent.

Even the serving of lunch takes on a different character. A business executive is accustomed to being waited on, but except for those few who have house servants—or wives willing to take on the daily chore of another meal—lunch in retirement is usually a self-prepared pickup, a warming up of designated leftovers, a collection of things assembled from the refrigerator, an improvised sandwich. Its significance is of an entirely different order: who prepares it, who cleans up afterward, and whether it creates any household problems ("You didn't tell me you used up the eggs").

One of the reasons the day seems to be longer for the retired person in the early months is that morning and afternoon run together without the lunchtime ritual as a substantial midday digression. The interaction with others is lost or greatly diminished, and the sense of being solitary is intensified. There is a carried-over response, now inappropriate but not yet entirely damped down, that says not having lunch with anyone is to be something of an outcast.

But more important, perhaps, in retirement men can no longer use lunchtime as the social device it always was: as one of the very few acceptable ways in which men can invite one another to become friends or form personal relationships with other men independent of their wives.

"Let's have lunch one day" is a recognizable social signal among men in the business world. Men can ask, "Are you free for lunch on Tuesday?" when they are unable to ask, "Can you help me?" It is far easier for a man to say, "So you like Italian food? Let me take you to my favorite place, Guido's," than to say, "Hey, maybe we have enough in common to be friends." It is one of the very few ways in which men's friendships—or alliances—are generated directly, without the intervention or the participation of women.

A man encountering a prospective friend in retirement is generally unable to follow this pattern. Women may invite each other to their homes for lunch, but for men to do so is felt to be suspect, awkward, and unseemly. So while there are other opportunities for male friendships, an important means of developing them is no longer available.

XIV. SHIFTING PERSPECTIVES

Our changing perceptions of time, security, struggle,
success, and failure.

IT CAN BE SEEN that the early stages of retirement are full
of new awareness, of familiar things seen from unfamiliar
angles.

One of these is a kind of reversal. All employees, executives or otherwise, contrive to make themselves as essential
as possible. The fact that the boss can't get along without
you is the essence of job security. But the art of retirement is
not only different, it is opposite. It is the art of making yourself unnecessary, of designing matters so that they can proceed without you, for this is the essence of freedom from the
dependence of others, the freedom that allows you to *not* do
whatever you don't feel like doing.

> *Notes from a retirement journal:* As I approach the end of a
> half-year in retirement, what captivates me most is the *open-*
> *endedness* of time, an experience quite new to me. All my
> life, anything I have ever done has had an end point or a
> stopping place; there was no such thing as unlimited time.
> Weekends always came to an end, and the work week began.
> The workday, however long, eventually was over. Vacations
> went quickly, illnesses slowly, but they always ended, and the
> normal cycle of time always resumed.
>   What I find strange is that I can do nothing at all, and

continue doing nothing as long as I please. And when I choose to stop doing nothing, there is no "normal" cycle of activity to resume; I can begin doing anything I want.

I have become conscious of having lived all my life in a structured time, whose shape and existence were so much part of my environment that I was really unconscious of it. Once outside that structure, I feel like an astronaut who goes outside his space vehicle—I become aware of the limitless expanse of alternatives, the enormousness of the "outside" universe.

I remember the profound shift of perspective I felt when on television I saw men on the moon. I remember going out of doors and looking up at the sky, and seeing the moon for the first time not as a celestial object, a thing in the sky, but as a *place.*

I remember the time when, after a lifelong fear of water, which had resulted in my being able to "swim" only by thrashing furiously, I suddenly and unaccountably found myself able to dive from the edge of the pool, find the bottom, open my eyes, and look around at the calm and silent place I had always feared. I wanted very much to sit quietly on the floor of the pool and enjoy the peace, but the pull of the surface was irresistible. No matter how hard I tried to stay down, I inexorably floated up. Up! A lifetime of being pulled down by gravity, of falling down when I let go, was suddenly reversed. When I discovered that to relax under water was to rise and that I floated when I stopped thrashing, stopped fighting to keep from "falling," stopped moving altogether, all my laws of falling and rising were suddenly reversed.

It is these instant insights, these new, unexpected, and unsuspected perceptions, that make lifelong impressions. They can never be forgotten; most important, they can never be reversed. I am no longer capable of seeing the moon as an object in the sky or of feeling myself as a weight that will fall to the bottom of a pool of water.

But I cannot accommodate to unstructured time.

I find myself constantly rebuilding the structure. I do

this by putting back the limits: I tell myself that I'll write for another half hour and then go to town and do my errands. I have not yet accepted the fact that I can write as long or as briefly as I please, and after that I can do something, or anything, or nothing.

My notes do not reveal the slightly scary quality of the feeling of unstructured time, the sense that I was not in phase with any cycle or rhythm outside myself. They do not reflect how uneasy I was made by the discovery that I could eat as many or as few meals as I pleased, have dinner at noon or at midnight or skip it altogether, that I could read for an hour or for ten hours, sleep late, rise early, or not get out of bed at all. I could go outside, stay inside, start, or stop, all as I chose and not because what I did fitted into any pattern that intersected with what the rest of the world was doing at the time.

This state was unendurable for me, and I cannot imagine anyone living comfortably this way for an extended period of time. So I exerted a good deal of energy on rebuilding a time frame, putting down psychological grids and coordinates on the map of the day, so that I could have a sense of where I am.

But the point here is that I now know that this time structure is man-made. More specifically, it is self-made. There is nothing that makes it really necessary except my anxiety at being without it. For me, it was a frightening excess of freedom, and it did not sit well until it was fettered and limited by self-imposed restraints, an inner voice that tells me I can't take a walk now because it's time to get ready for dinner.

In contrast, a friend expressed a different feeling about time in a letter he wrote me a year after he had retired: "Where the heck has time gone? When I try to account for it, I cannot—nothing seems to have happened. I think I've become accustomed to the spaces between periods of activity

—I'm getting very good at just doing nothing. Despite my previous experience with inactivity—that it makes time drag on very slowly—my present experience in retirement is just the opposite. Inactivity makes the days fly by in a blur. I don't have to accomplish anything. I don't have a sense of falling behind, of wasting time. Nor do I feel guilty. I'm just astonished at *how quickly nothing is happening.*"

If time creates a problem of internal measurement, achievement creates another. We think of our actions as having some cumulative effect that enables us to measure how much we have accomplished. We need to feel that we are making headway. The ways in which we do this are varied and are wiped out by retirement.

In our careers, most of us use the common analogy of climbing a ladder. It is a ladder with very approximate and uncertain dimensions, but we do know when we have taken a step up, we can recognize reaching a higher rung, whatever form that may take. It may be as unmistakable as a promotion or as subtle as an improvement in organizing one's time, but our constant and intuitive self-awareness readily identifies it as progress and as a benchmark from which to take the next measurement.

However, in retirement—certainly in the early days—there does not seem to be any continuity; the things we do or take pride in are not cumulative, we do not get a feeling of progression. Without it, we may know we have done some things well, but not in a way that can be ordered into any kind of sequence.

The range of possible achievements is infinite, of course. It could include finding a good tax-free investment for the final bonus payment, learning how to make a good pot of soup, starting a jogging program, and getting at least one letter written a day. The point is that *they do not add up*; they are isolated events. The consequence is not a sense of moving forward; it feels more like milling around.

A different observation about achievement was made to me this way, "One of the ways in which retirement impacted on me was when I suddenly realized that I had come to a point when I could no longer fail. All during my working life, and my school life before it, failure was always a possibility —not imminent, perhaps, but certainly possible. I could flunk an exam or an entire course, and I could be fired from my job. It might be my own fault or not, it could be just or unfair, but the fact was I was always at risk, there was always a way I could be disqualified, thrown out of school, or thrown out of work. I didn't go around worrying about it or live in fear and suspense. It was just a realistic awareness that there is no such thing as permanent security.

"But when I retired on an assured pension, I realized I actually had found permanent security. My welfare was no longer dependent on what I did or what I was, on my judgment, on my reputation, or on my ability, on who liked me and who didn't. I was beyond employability and no one would ever again have the power to fire me."

It was the same man who, on another occasion, expressed the opposite idea, unaware of the relationship between the two. "The thing I miss most is the opportunity to succeed, to score some sort of victory that my peers and my business associates would consider really worthwhile. For instance, in a one-week visit to our subsidiary in Tokyo I was able to put my finger on exactly what was wrong with the business and come back with a program for turning it around. There just is no way in retirement to do anything like that."

It seemed to me that he had said first that in retirement he was beyond failure, and then that in retirement he was beyond success, although he did not link the two ideas. And contained in his second example was reference to another kind of loss that is generally overlooked when people think of retirement: the fact that so many of us operate at our best only in circumstances we cannot provide for ourselves in retirement. Just as a symphony conductor must have an orchestra in order to express his talents, those of us from the corporate world can express ours only in the place from which we have now been permanently exiled.

There is no way an attorney who is expert in antitrust litigation can use his skills or get satisfaction from them when he leaves the business world—it is the only world in which antitrust litigation exists. The people involved in mergers and acquisitions, public stock offerings, proxy fights, international banking, economic forecasting, corporate personnel policy, worldwide information networks, and all the other complexities of the corporate world can find nothing like them in private life.

Another man, a personnel executive who did make the connection between the two ideas, commented: "It's a strange feeling. I'm not sure how to deal with it. The best analogy I can give you is that I feel like a powerful electromagnet, with the current turned off. My work has always been the current that energized and polarized me. When that stopped, I was cut off from my energy source. I no longer had polarity. Maybe I should explain that. Magnets—which is why I use that analogy—have two opposite poles. One attracts, the other repels. They are as opposite as success and failure, which is really what I am talking about. When I say that I lost my polarity, I mean that without work there is no succeeding and no failing. It's all one neutral field. It is static, uniform. There is no force, no energy in it."

I think he was also saying that without polarity there is no orientation—no direction. Which is another way of saying there is no clear purpose or goal. Moving in any direction changes little or nothing; one may as well stand still. This stasis comes not, as is often said, from lack of interests or hobbies or from the fact that people are not good company for themselves. More often it comes from secure retirement, which brings us to a place where there are no ups and downs. Which seems to suggest the paradox that security brings its own hazards.

XV. MOVING AWAY

How people choose where to live in retirement.

MUCH RETIREMENT PLANNING deals with choosing a place to retire to. Perhaps a third of those who retire these days move to other places, and the proportion is higher in middle-class retirement. The vast majority of the retired people I have met are no longer living where the husband pursued his career and the couple raised their children. There are many practical reasons for changing living arrangements at retirement: the shrunken family, elimination of the need to live within reach of the office, greater prudence about expenses, the attraction of a more temperate climate, these come to mind at once.

There is also the sense of flux, of making a complete change, of starting anew, that stimulates the desire for a new environment. The linking of retirement to the vacation-leisure-recreation concept makes it inappropriate to continue living in the heart of a big city or even a crowded suburb. In some cases, I am sure, the question of why one should move is never closely examined. A new freedom has been offered for the first time, a freedom to live wherever one pleases, and it seems to follow that this new option should be exercised.

One can actually go shopping for answers to "where to retire," but it is not possible to shop among the various life-styles from which one might choose the answer to "how." But mostly I think people who find it difficult to deal with the idea of retiring are able to use the process of researching possible communities for retirement as a compromise. It enables them to feel busy making plans and arrangements, although they may really be keeping busy in order to avoid making them. It also provides an easy way to bring up the subject, for one spouse to send the other the message, "We must begin to plan and talk about retiring." It is often done with "Here's an ad for a [Florida condominium] [camper] [retirement village]. Maybe we ought to take a look at it." Thus the long journey into retirement is begun.

The things that seem important in arriving at a decision about where to live have surprisingly little relationship to the things that prove important afterward. Almost universally, weather is a major consideration. But something tells me that "indoor people" who see themselves as theater-goers, readers, gourmet cooks, good conversationalists, and music lovers would not ordinarily consider climate to be the major consideration in choosing a place to live. The cultural facilities and the people in the community would be much more likely to be important. But this does not seem to happen—it's weather that dominates the list.

There is a fundamental assumption that retirement means spending more time outdoors. Whenever I have asked why, the question has been brushed aside as foolish. Usually there is a reference to the need for older people to live in warmer climates, the fact that a longer outdoor season is necessary for enough sailing, swimming, golf, or fishing, and so on. My skepticism comes from my knowledge that the people who make these statements are often those who deny any identification as "older people" and who sail, golf, or fish in all kinds of weather. It seems to me that the emphasis on climate conceals more than it reveals.

The second major consideration is money—the need or desire to be prudent on a fixed income, even though that income may be ample. Selling the family home and realizing the accrued inflationary profit often provides the capital to finance important aspects of the retirement program. But in almost every such program, there is the idea of lowering expenses, of moving to a place where the cost of living is less.

The third major consideration is much less definite and emphatic; it usually has to do with proximity to something or someone. "I won't be too far from my daughter, and I'll be able to get to see the grandchildren a few times a year," or "I'll be midway between Charles and Louise and will be able to visit both." Sometimes it's, "Some of my friends have moved down there, so there will be people we know," and "It's only forty miles from the university, and I expect to spend a good deal of time there," or "When we're bored, we're only an hour away from the capital, and we can go to the shows and restaurants." One has the feeling that these are afterthoughts, rather than considerations that played a decisive part in the selection.

I am impressed by the fact that the answer to "where" is generally based on these few elements—climate, cost, proximity—which do not seem to be crucial. The logic often seems to be faulty—the man who moved to a place where he didn't have to shovel snow four months a year is now mowing his lawn nine months a year; the man who wanted to live in the Sunshine State now is careful to avoid exposure to the sun; the man who sought to reduce his overhead is living in an expensive, new condominium.

XVI. THE SOCIAL NETWORK

The unsettling experience of finding your place and making new relationships in a strange community.

COMPARED WITH THE THINGS people worry about in choosing a new community, what actually turns out to be significant is surprising. Perhaps the greatest problem is the many-faceted one of being a newcomer in the community.

Even families that have moved without difficulty in the past find that relocation on retirement involves new and special problems. Previously, the husband was able to form new relationships readily at the office, as could the wife at her job, at the PTA, or in other volunteer activities; the children made friends at school or play.

But a retired couple whose children are grown and away do not have such common ground for meeting others. For some people the church or synagogue provides sufficient opportunity for compatible new relationships, but those whose religious affiliation has never been strong discover very quickly that they lack the social network in which they used to have automatic membership: the network of fellow workers, or parent/child activities, of old friends and neighbors, and local causes. In retrospect, this greatly enhances the value of the network left behind and increases the realization of loss.

It is no longer possible to call an old friend at six o'clock and invite him to play bridge after dinner. One cannot ring the neighbor's doorbell while going by just to say hello. "It's not merely that there's no one to share gossip with," a woman told me, "it's that I don't know any gossip, because I don't know anyone well enough yet."

Newcomers generally recognize they must make a special effort to meet other people and make new friends. They join organizations even if they have not been joiners and go to the meetings even if they are of little interest. They attend lectures, classes, workshops, teas, walking tours, potlucks, dinner theater groups—any event that brings them in contact with other people. Some of the attraction is the opportunity to do things they may never before have had time to do, but the greater motive often is the opportunity to meet people.

Some make a practice of striking up conversations wherever they go, with people on the bus, at the Laundromat, in the adjoining seat at the theater, in the waiting line at the restaurant. But this is an indiscriminate and random search pattern; it often leads to nothing more than a polite exchange of superficialities, a ritual in which two strangers politely and cheerfully agree with each other and then go on about their separate affairs.

Some people find it difficult or impossible to take the initiative in forming new friendships or making a suitable place for themselves in the community. They are genuinely shy, and don't want to be seen as pushy; they wait to be asked and, when they are overlooked, withdraw further. Others simply don't want to make the effort or find it too unpleasant and tend to remain isolated. They can often persuade themselves that they prefer it this way, that they are self-sufficient, value their privacy, and prefer to be left alone.

Whatever the mode of adaptation may be, the newcomer knows that every encounter offers possibilities. "The meeting ritual is like a strange form of courtship," I was told. "Each tries to make a quick judgment about whether the other is worth the effort. It is a judgment based on limited information: how people are dressed, how they speak, where they come from, how old they are or appear to be. Almost always this first impression is wrong. If you get to know him better, you find the flip old gent who looked like a chemistry professor owns a food shop and the gentle, soft-spoken lady taught pathology at the university. The monosyllabic fellow you thought was a fruit farmer turns out to have been a newspaper editor, and the one who made that witty remark proves to be a scatterbrain who was quoting something he had read. But there is no alternative—you have to try and keep trying, because there is no way of knowing whether or not you are at the beginning of a new friendship."

Friendship. The word must be given a new definition, one discovers. It has always meant a certain intimacy, trust, and acceptance based on a history of shared experience. It is a relationship with roots deep in the past. In retirement, you learn that this definition applies only to the "old" friendships, the ones you have left behind. The new friendships have a different quality and character, for they have no roots and no history. They involve little intimacy and not much trust.

In such new friendships there are large areas that on a map would be labeled *terra incognita*. Even after months or years, you may never know why your new friend and his first wife were divorced after thirty-two years or how he met the woman to whom he is now married. You can make only a vague guess about his income level and the state of his health, never get a hint as to why he goes to Jonesboro every Thursday, why he gets letters from his son but not from his daughter, and why he gave up his medical practice in his early fifties. If this kind of information is not volunteered in these later-life friendships, one does not ask.

But what is done, in contrast, is to offer credentials. "One of the things I found we were doing," a woman told me, "was developing a sort of shorthand description of ourselves, because the occasion of the first or second meeting with a new couple was always, one way or another, an exchange of credentials. Listening to myself answering questions about Jack and me, I realized how much editing was necessary in order not to give an incorrect impression. If I first spoke of my work, it was assumed that Jack's job was not as important. If I spoke of belonging to the church, it was assumed that we were devout, and if I told of my education it was a signal that we were 'intellectuals.' Every clue was given weight, even if it had none, and the total effect of all the clues was to so distort the image of ourselves as to constitute almost outright misinformation.

"What we learned to do was to sprinkle the clues in the right sequence and with the proper degree of emphasis, to omit the misleading ones and highlight those that would open up the conversation. It was the social equivalent of being interviewed for a job, and we had to learn the best pattern of responses to such inevitable opening gambits as 'Where do you come from?' and 'What do you do?' "

She went on, "We soon learned not to refer to anything that required explanation, because there often was no time or opportunity to explain; in brief encounters, it is essential to help the other person classify you quickly and properly if you are ever going to get beyond the introduction."

Newcomers in the community soon learn how quickly the classifying and sorting are done. "She asked me if I play bridge and when I said I didn't play cards, she said, 'Oh, that's too bad,' as though I had some sort of disability, and started talking to someone else."

There is a lot of quick matching up at this stage, and many people learn to play card for card:

"Do you have children?"

"Yes, two. Do you?"

"We have a son on the West Coast. And two lovely grandchildren."

"Our children are still unmarried. But I have a brother on the West Coast, in Los Angeles."

"My son is in Sacramento. He's a research chemist."

"Really? John taught chemistry for many years."

This kind of exchange can be sustained for quite a while, but is usually abandoned if nothing of particular interest is disclosed on either side in the first few minutes.

Another situation: "At home, our telephone was always ringing. I used to think it was a nuisance, until I realized that Mary and I had been reading in the living room for two whole evenings and the phone hadn't rung once. I asked myself whose call I was expecting, and I realized that we really didn't know anyone in town who would have occasion to call us at home in the evening. It was a very lonely feeling; I wasn't used to it."

And when the phone did ring, it was Mrs. Butner. "You remember, we met at the church supper. Harry and I are going to the film at the public library, and we wondered if you would like to join us."

Hurried conference. "Which one was she? Oh, the one from Illinois. White hair, loves astrology, two grandchildren. I don't want to see an old film at the library. Okay, you're right, we can't start refusing invitations.

"Mrs. Butner? Mary and I would love to join you."

So the newcomer finds himself accepting invitations he would formerly have declined, joining organizations in which he had no prior interest, engaging in activities to which he had never been drawn, making friends with people he may not really like.

"After a while I realized it was absurd to expect to find people I'd like as much as those I've known for years. And other people weren't likely to see me as their ideal choice, either. In a sense, we were all compromising in accepting one another, at least to begin with. I kept thinking how easy it used to be to talk with my friends back home. They knew me so well I didn't have to explain myself, justify my opinions, clarify what I was saying, be careful to avoid giving wrong impressions. Whatever I said, they usually knew what I meant. And whatever they said I could readily put into the context of everything we knew about each other. It's tough to try to get close to people who haven't the vaguest idea of the kind of person you are."

This process of lowered expectations in new relationships implies a certain humility, induced in large part by the uncertainty of living, however temporarily, without a sustaining social network while learning how to construct one.

You can never be certain of how much value will be placed on you by others. "I found myself offering various aspects of myself in quick succession, not knowing how much any of them was worth. It was like trying to collect credits or Brownie points, not knowing the value system. I knew my appearance made the important first impression. I had never before had any problem deciding what to wear. But people dress differently here—there seems to be a definite dress code, although a more informal one.

"I knew that the way I smiled on being introduced, the ease with which I struck up a conversation, the way I was able to express myself, were all going into my rating. I was aware that these people knew nothing about me except what they were able to observe for themselves—they could not know that I had a good sense of humor until I made some clever or witty remark; they could not tell that I had a good mind until I made an intelligent observation.

"Meanwhile, with another part of my mind, I was scanning the room for those people I might like and who might like me. When this happened, there would be an exchange of signals that marked the beginning of a very delicate social minuet, each of us going only as far as we were sure it would be safe, and ready to retreat if we realized we had made an error of judgment. There was no outright assertion, for example, of political views or contentious opinions. They were offered very tentatively and in their most moderate form; if they met with agreement, I felt I could go a shade further, then another step, and so on."

It is generally easy to recognize when the test period is over; there is a relaxation of the formalities, although the relationship rarely becomes close or as intimate as an "old" friendship. It usually remains more casual, less intense, less open; one puts less weight on it, makes less of an emotional investment in it, and expects less from it.

Meanwhile, what of the "old" friendships? They do not all wither and die, but they change drastically. Communication shifts to new channels: letters, cards, snapshots, long distance calls. Coming together is no longer casual; meetings require planning and coordination. Most of all, they work differently.

A visit now is much more than dropping in—it frequently means moving in as houseguests.

"Jill and I felt very comfortable with Robert and his wife in almost every kind of social situation for many years. But after we moved away, we had our first experience of actually living in their home with them, and then our first experience of having them live in ours when they returned our visit. I was amazed at how differently people relate to each other when one is a guest in the other's home. It wasn't bad, and it worked out okay, but we were—all four of us—conscious that the flow was different from the way it used to be."

Another man, talking about his family, said, "He's been my older brother all my life—for sixty-five years. Yet there never was any occasion for either of us to sleep in the other's home—we both lived in the same neighborhood all our lives. When he and my sister-in-law came to visit us, I got a very peculiar feeling; it seemed odd to have them in the guest room, to see how they prepared for bed and got up in the morning; I felt strange showing them the town I lived in, introducing them to my new circle of friends, showing them how I spent my time. It was almost as though they were strangers I was trying to make feel at home—and I think that Jerry felt just as odd having Sue and me stay with him."

It takes several months to build a social network in a new community, and it is an ordeal most people would not like to repeat. The social network I have discussed is a system of interpersonal relationships among a dozen or so people. You can find a place in such a social system more readily than you can find your place in the community as a whole.

Those who have lived in their home community for a number of years acquire in time a degree of public recognition in an area wider than their social circle. Individuals become recognized as "leaders" and attain high visibility; they are known as being responsive to community causes and are generally solicited to help or participate in them. It takes a lot of living in a new community even to learn what forces are at play and what issues are of concern, much less to position oneself in relation to them. Meanwhile, one seems to have *no* place in the community, good or bad. As in the period when one is trying to form a new social network, this is a time of disorientation, with feelings of *not belonging*. It is much more difficult to overcome.

A retired pediatrician from Westchester said, "Back home, people used to call me to discuss what was going on, to ask my opinion about things. When a piece of private property was coming onto the market, someone would generally let me know in advance in case I wanted to make the investment. When the new shopping mall was in trouble, I was one of the people called in to discuss how to get it straightened out, even though I knew nothing about retailing. I was simply known as a guy with a good mind, and with integrity, whatever that is. When our city councilman wanted to test his bill to outlaw the massage parlor at the edge of town, I was one of the people he called for an opinion. People were interested in who I was going to vote for, and why."

What this man missed most in his new community was this sense of recognition, of respect, this acknowledgment of his presence. "I've become chairman of one fund drive here, and my wife is heading another. I'm on the board of directors of two of the community voluntary agencies. I go to all the town meetings. But that does not seem to do it—people don't call me with inside information, no one really wants to know my opinions, I'm simply not a part of the inner circle—and I'm not even sure who is."

An echo of this can be heard from another direction. "I know it doesn't seem important but in my hometown the butcher knew me, the dry cleaner and I had finally reached an understanding of what I meant by 'spotless,' and the manager at the supermarket knew my checks were always good and that I preferred to buy eggs a half-dozen at a time even though it meant splitting a carton. I had gone to the same doctor for over thirty years and to the same dentist for almost as long. The optician knew I came in about once a month to have my eyeglass frames adjusted, and the fellow in the shoe store didn't have to be reminded about the padding in the heel of my right shoe when I came in for a new pair. The man in the photo shop sold me the camera I own and never had to ask what kind of film I wanted. I knew exactly where to put the trash for collection, and the mailman knew my son-in-law's name when mail came for him at my address."

She went on, "None of this seemed very important until it all ended suddenly—just like that. In our new community, there was a double problem—not only didn't I know anyone; no one knew me. I had to try to find a good dry cleaner, a new butcher, doctor, dentist. The young shoe salesman told me I didn't need padding in my shoes, and I didn't feel comfortable asking to have my eyeglasses adjusted again and again as a favor. I had to bring in my camera to find out what film it required, and was given some I had never used before. The old-shoe feeling of being in my right place was gone, and instead I felt stiff and creaky, awkward and out of place, and incredibly dependent on people who were strangers to me and, even worse, to whom I wasn't anybody at all."

I know it's not true for all women, but it seems to me that in retirement women generally do better than men at finding ways to feel more comfortable in new surroundings. Unlike men, even women accustomed to going to work every day can usually find reassurance in familiar activities in the home, whereas household routines do not serve this purpose for most men.

A man told me, "I noticed that when my wife was feeling homesick, lonesome, or out of place—she called it feeling uneasy—she'd rearrange the kitchen utensils or go through the closets or attack the mildew on the bathroom tiles. The way she polished silver when she was in these moods reminded me of the way some people rub worry beads. I envied the way she could make a little island for herself, wherever she was, by doing things that gave her a sense of continuity. Outside the house, she was able to plug into community activities much more readily than I could.

"It's different for me. My familiar world requires a desk, business papers, a secretary, a telephone, an appointment calendar. I never did much of anything on a regular basis around the house back home, so I don't have household stuff to fall back on down here. I set up a study in the spare room, but except for bills and other financial transactions I don't have anything to work on, nothing to dictate, no phone calls, no meetings. When I got six cartons of papers that were shipped to me from my old office, I had a real ball. I enjoyed a whole week of arranging and filing them, and I was sorry when the job was done."

A woman said, "Right after we moved here, I began going to a brown bag lunch at 'A Woman's Place' once a week. Every Wednesday I'd take along a cup of yogurt or some fruit and cheese and spend a couple of hours with a group of women, who, like me, wanted other women's company. My husband thinks of it as some kind of meeting, but it's just a friendly time for women to be together. Some are in their twenties, others in their seventies, and all ages in between. Some are strangers, others come often; no one knows everyone. We sit and talk. Sometimes the discussion gets heated, but most of the time it's just relaxing conversation, friendly, and—for me—most supportive. I don't know why men don't do the same kind of thing."

Some retired men are beginning to get together for more than poker games or TV football, but they still shy away from such terms as "support group" and tend to talk mostly about business, sports, investments, and politics because they haven't learned how to share their feelings, doubts, and insecurity.

What it comes down to is that people who relocate are displaced—in their social circle, neighborhood, and community. They never completely recapture the "old-shoe feeling" of being permanently and comfortably settled in, nor do they ever fully reconstruct the kind of social network they left behind. "I discovered what I should have known but didn't: that there is no substitute for time, that having friends and a place in the community is a function not simply of personality but primarily of *time*. Once you cut down the full-grown tree, there is no way it can be entirely replaced in your lifetime; there just isn't enough time left."

It is notable to me that none of the people who relocated at retirement fully realized the profound and irrevocable change they were making and the ways in which they would be affected by it.

XVII. THE "FEMININE" WORLD OF RETIREMENT

In retirement, men feel they are entering more of a woman's world; men and women seem to exercise power and authority differently.

WHETHER OR NOT retirement involves relocation, it does involve dislocation. I have already commented on the many forms that takes, but there is one respect in which it seems to me to be profound, recognized instantly by any retired man, yet almost never discussed. I am referring to the perceived feminization of the world of the retired man, the simple fact that whereas the world of business is primarily a masculine one, the world of the retired is seen primarily as a feminine one. Feminine, partly because it is populated by many more women than men but mostly because it is a social world and this makes it seem a woman's domain, if only for the reason that before retirement men spend so much less time in it than women do.

That it is populated by more women than men has far less to do with retirement than with aging. The disparity in the life-spans of men and women becomes visible at this stage of life; almost any gathering of people over sixty is a group in which women outnumber men. Of the more than 20 million people over sixty-five in 1970, only 8.4 million were men.

So the retired man's sense of living in a female world is formed in part by the fact that men are usually outnumbered, and so constitute a minority, and in part from the fact that the man has made an abrupt crossover from a world in which exactly the opposite is true.

Here we are dealing more with perceptions than with statistics. It may be statistically true that American Telephone & Telegraph employs more women than men, but the company is seen as a male enterprise created and controlled by men.

Further, in most business organizations the higher up in the company hierarchy the fewer women we see. So the middle- and upper-management executive operates in what is visibly a man's world, despite the large numbers of women who may be employed at lower levels of the same companies. The world from which the executive comes, when he enters retirement, is one in which men predominate, not only in visible numbers but also in power.

The world he enters is populated differently. And power, or what he sees as power, is distributed differently and displayed differently. I have previously commented on the ways the executive is alert to power signals in the business world. In his sudden transition into retirement, he continues to receive and interpret power signals, although they come from entirely different sources, more specifically from his wife and the increased number of women around him. Many of these signals make him uneasy; he feels the suspicion and alertness of an animal that has wandered into another's territory. He does not feel himself to be on home ground or even on neutral turf.

Now that he is home to stay, whose turf is it? It has been his wife's mostly—now it may be theirs—but it certainly is not simply his. The ways in which men deal with this matter of territoriality tells us not only how retirement affects men but also how the business world has conditioned them. I will discuss the latter aspect presently, but first, let's look at the transition period.

One man referred to a teacher-student relationship: "My wife knows how things are done; this is her territory—she knows the right behavior in the Laundromat, how to deal with the people in the supermarket, where things go in the kitchen, what the right thing is to make for the covered-dish supper. She knows the etiquette for whether to invite Mary Jones to move over to our table at the luncheonette, and whether or not I should pick up her check. She listens to my suggestions, but she is the one who arranges our social life, makes the dates, knows whom to invite with whom. I respect her authority in all of this."

Her authority—perhaps that is a major clue. To the executive still sensitive to his loss of power, women do seem to act more authoritatively, to show their power more openly, to seem more dominant, assertive, functional. They certainly seem to feel more "at home" than he does.

To a man feeling powerless, this can be felt as threatening, for in the business world power has a clear purpose: to achieve domination. An executive still fresh from the business wars has learned not to trust others to use their power benignly, and it is impossible for him to accept the fact that perhaps they are not using it at all or even thinking in such terms.

What we are dealing with here is his perception, for where we are determines what we see. We must also take into account perceptions other than his. His wife may be growing more aware of her own strength, her consciousness raised to the fact that today's women do have power, or have more power than they thought, and that they can exert it in their own behalf in their own lives. Perhaps the word "power" is a misleading word, for men and women seem to define it differently by using it in different contexts, men as enabling command of others and women as enabling command of themselves. Another widening feminine perception is that men —particularly men in retirement—are less powerful, more vulnerable, and more readily challenged than women may have formerly believed.

In an ideal world, these changing perceptions make for a better balance and lay the necessary foundations for a more equitable relationship by converting the concept of power used to dominate another to that of strength shared for mutual good. In the long run, after the earlier conditioning has been overcome, this often turns out to be the way the relationship is reshaped—perhaps the only way it can be properly reshaped. But this lies in the future. In the short run, in the process of becoming retired, there is a period of badly garbled signals, poor transmission, bad reception, and mistaken interpretation, with kernels of truth scattered in a pool of misinformation. While so much of a man's reading of these signals is a conditioned one, inappropriately carried over from an entirely different context, some of it is accurate, for a woman in transition is as unpredictable as a man in transition; a woman, like a man, is capable of using power for domination.

This may come down to what James Thurber used to call The War Between Men and Women; a great deal of it extends far beyond the reach of a discussion of men's retirement. And much of it hinges on the way in which particular men and women have developed their relationship with each other long before retirement entered the picture. But some parts seem pertinent as illustrating the kinds of perceptions men have of women and of the "feminine" world in the course of adjusting to retirement.

Having left the office for the last time, the man begins to examine in greater detail the world in which he will spend the rest of his life. For the first time he can see what his home, his neighborhood, and other people's lives have been like while he was away at work. He begins to explore his small world like a visitor. His wife shows him how she does things, where things go, what happens during the day. He may be amused, bored, or fascinated, but he may also get the feeling of a newcomer being given a tour of the establishment by the old-time resident. At the same time, he learns the rules (get the garbage out before noon on Mondays and Thursdays, it's okay to accept a package for the neighbors from United Parcel but not a C.O.D. from the mailman, we do the laundry on Tuesdays).

Outside the home, he feels that he and other men are somehow more visible. In any gathering, even in the lobby during the concert intermission, there are usually fewer men than women, so to him the men are more obvious. The women tend to talk to one another and to visit the ladies' room together, while the men tend to be less animated, less talkative, often just listening politely to the women's conversation.

As he explores the new environment, he notes how different it is from the world of business in which he has usually spent his time. In any new environment, it is the differences that stand out; the similarities are less significant. If he goes for a walk during the day, he passes women on their way to and from a variety of household and personal errands and men who work out of doors—telephone repair crews, sanitation workers, street repavers, police. He sees women tending preschool children, a convalescent sitting in the sun, children out of school for no apparent reason, people who look as though they should be at work, possibly unemployed. He sees salesmen shuffling papers in their cars before making their calls, meter readers, canvassers. Occasionally an older man sitting quietly, lost in some reverie. For some men, this experience generates a pervasive sense of disconnection, of having no relationship to anything around them, the feeling that they are in the wrong place, don't really belong here, without knowing where they do belong. "I know it sounds strange," one man told me, "but I imagine it's something like the feeling of being . . ." Here he looked at me, dubious of my ability to understand what he was saying. ". . . the feeling of being shipwrecked."

I tried to supply the rest of the image for him. "Cast up on some foreign shore, without having a way to get back home?" He nodded.

For some reason, his image evoked a long-buried memory of mine when, in my early twenties, I contracted tuberculosis and suddenly found myself in bed in the contagious ward of the hospital. I was filled with dread, not of my own condition but of being exposed to the other patients in the same room. They had the same disease I had, and I was the sickest of the lot, but I could not for a long while rid myself of the feeling that this place was dangerous; it was *the wrong place to be.*

What was wrong was not the place but the new relationship I had acquired to it.

As the retired man wanders through his familiar neighborhood, seeing it now with changed perceptions, he begins to understand the group of oldsters playing checkers in the park, the fellows who hang around the firehouse, the ones who watch the high school baseball team practicing in the school yard. For the first time, it occurs to him that these groups may be comprised not merely of people who don't seem to have anything else to do—their significance may be that they are groups of *men* and that it is not just the interest in checkers or in baseball that keeps them together but the need or desire to form a male community, however makeshift, however temporary.

At home, his wife may now share with him many of what were always considered to be her chores—the things he didn't have time for when he was busy earning a living, the household problems he would have found annoying, the errands that had to be run during the workday. Now she seems to have the major responsibilities, and he has the time to help her.

In the retirement world, we see men in supermarkets with shopping lists, men doing family laundry in the Laundromats, men taking clothes to the cleaner. The more recently retired often feel that they are helping their wives; it takes quite a while for the retired executive to think of them as common tasks, as much his now as hers. They are what the business world considers "service and maintenance tasks," respectable and necessary, but not calling for great skill, or "productive." To the operating executive, they are what other people do. To the male executive, they are what women usually do. In retirement, it is not the tasks, but his relationship to them that has changed.

All behavior carries a message, and most messages, however intended, have a consequence. Consider this familiar sight in the supermarket: The woman is doing the shopping, the man follows, pushing the shopping cart. In the few conversations in which I have raised the question of why both go to market, I have been told, "Well, we decide what to get" and "It's good for him to get to know how to shop—and what things cost."

Plausible as that may be, I don't think that many women realize the hidden message men can and do read into this behavior. What some men hear is, "I'm teaching him what I know," and others hear, "I'm teaching him that I know more than he does."

There is a school of accepted social humor represented by the stories women tell about the way their retired husbands bumble and fumble simple household tasks; these are generally told with a dash of humor and a slightly concealed cutting edge. Men who have negotiated the purchase and sale of merchandise and property all their lives seem never to master properly the skill of buying fruit: "It's ridiculous to pay that price for oranges!" or "It's too early for peaches—in a couple of weeks they'll be half the price," or "These are cooking apples; I'll have to show you which are eating apples."

Wives who may think they know their husbands very well may fail to realize that in the business world messages such as these are attacks. Men who intellectually understand that these messages are certainly not so intended nevertheless feel as though they are. These feelings are to be concealed—as most men's feelings are—because there is no way to express the felt reaction without seeming foolish or overreactive. But when men do get together, the generated hostility readily emerges in matching stories.

In such a group, a man who could make a fine carburetor adjustment and stop the water drip from the air conditioner told sarcastically of how he was taken back again and again over the living room rug and shown the failings in his vacuum cleaning: "You see here?" he mimicked his wife's voice. "You've got to run it right along the baseboard, this way. The way you're doing it leaves marks on the wall. Can't you see them? You're not blind!" We all knew he was talking about more than cleaning a rug—he was talking about changing relationships and hidden messages.

Some of these messages, as I have said, may contain kernels of truth. In the changing relationship at retirement, some women may have stumbled upon a safe way to express concealed resentments and hostility they may have felt during thankless years of cooking, cleaning, and shopping. While now enjoying the benefit of their husband's help, they may sense a long-delayed justice in being able to criticize the way *he* cooks or cleans or shops.

The situation is intensified if the wife, perhaps because

she is younger, bored, "liberated," ambitious, or simply wants to bring more money into the house, has a job. I have spoken to some of the resultant "house husbands," as one of them referred to himself. On the days his wife works, he is in charge and responsible for the household and for getting dinner on the table. Yet, when she arrives, tired from work, his role turns ambiguous. "I try to tune in to her mood when she comes in the door. Sometimes she just wants to be the homecoming worker, to sit down and have dinner, and to take it easy in the evening. Then I know I'll do the serving, clearing away, washing up. At other times, she'll just take over the kitchen from me, reseason the food, tell me not to make corn when I make potatoes, serve the meal, but expect me to clean up. And after I wash the dishes, she'll putter around in the kitchen for an hour, rearranging the things in the refrigerator, making out a new shopping list, and scouring the sink that seemed clean to me. It takes a lot of my nervous energy to follow all the ins and outs, making the proper responses, and keep peace without arguments."

Another man felt he had analyzed the situation more deeply. "She is in a sense taking over my former role as the workingman. But she doesn't want to be trapped in it as I always was—she wants to step out of it at will. At the same time, she doesn't want to return to the role she formerly had, as the housewife, but she doesn't want to give it up, either. She is keeping her options open, to be in my former role or in hers, or in any mixture of them that serves her purpose at the moment. So she oscillates unpredictably between them. The problem is that the only role I have is whatever one she is not playing, so I too keep swinging back and forth, not to serve my purposes but to serve hers. And that builds up a lot of resentment that I have no good way to express. I often get the feeling that when she comes home, I'm pretty okay and she's uptight. By the end of the evening, she has unwound and I am the one who is all tensed up." The husband seemed unaware of the implication of role reversal in his account; before he retired, he may have expected her to sense and accommodate to his moods in just this way when he came home from work.

The man may begin to reply to some of their personal correspondence, a function she always handled. Now he finds himself writing letters to old friends as the spokesman for the couple. "I haven't written a letter in longhand in over twenty years—I always dictated correspondence to my secretary. It seems odd to be writing a letter to Jack, who lived next door to us for so long. We talked on the phone or across the yard for fifteen years, but I never had occasion to write him a letter. When I got one from him, I was surprised to see what his handwriting looked like; I had never seen it before."

If it's not social correspondence, it may be horticulture, gourmet cookery, or yoga. The man sees himself following his wife into areas of her interests and activities. It suggests sexism to describe these as being feminine, but this obscures the fact that he has always identified them as being her interests, not his, and his perception is that he is beginning to share her life in a way that only her women friends have done. The operational term to him is that it is *her* life; it does not feel like a new life they are creating together. And, because it is hers, he sees her as having become the primary partner.

In many couple relationships, perhaps in most, one of the partners may see the other as the primary or leading one, but is not too much concerned about it. The factors that are special to the retirement adjustment are, first, that when the man is accustomed to seeing himself in this leading role, he generally has a difficult time when he feels the roles have become reversed; second, because it is a strange perspective, he sees the unaccustomed disparity as being greater than it may actually be; and, finally, that his perception may be accurate if his wife finds her ascendancy in the new relationship too gratifying or a way of righting former wrongs. The pendulum sometimes swings too far in such adjustments, but in time a more equitable balance is usually restored. What has occurred is really a collision between the culture of the business world and that of private life. In time, when both partners inhabit what will become their common culture, these differences in their attitudes and perceptions will diminish.

The result may be the development of entirely new perspectives in both partners—in a way, the development of a culture new to both of them. In this new culture it will be possible for the man to see his wife, and women generally, as equals without feeling threatened by their equality. This is an attitude quite different from seeing women as having grown suddenly more powerful or from "granting" them equality. And his wife can see herself as a whole person sharing many aspects of her life with a partner who is fully present. They can see each other as sharing strength and giving it, rather than using it.

When we see a retired couple who have worked their way through to the other side of the problem, we can admire their air of quiet confidence, their absence of neurotic responses, their constructive use of emotional energy, all of which suggest the extraordinary possibilities that can emerge in retirement when the influence of the culture of the business world is no longer felt in the home.

XVIII. TOGETHERNESS

At retirement, most marriages require a changed balance between separation and togetherness, dependency and autonomy.

WHATEVER RELATIONSHIP EMERGES during the early period of retirement, whether or not it reflects the desire and intention for equality, for sharing, and for erasing sex distinctions, the result is generally a loss of separateness, less you-and-me and more us-and-we. The relationship starts becoming homogenized, and the coupling becomes a merging. At the extreme, the two become one; they do everything in unison; one is rarely seen without the other. They hold all opinions in common, speak for each other, and it is impossible to deal with either as a separate person. This merging is a familiar sight, taken by some people as evidence of remarkable devotion. To describe the pair as "inseparable" may be intended to express admiration or envy, but only by those who fail to see that the same adjective applies to Siamese twins.

Such merging in retirement usually means the collapse of one personality into the other. It may be defined as surrender on one side or as total domination on the other. Whichever occurs, the result is not a doubling, but a halving. Where there were two personalities, there remains only one. Where there were two wills, there is now a single will. Where each takes strength from the other, the total strength of each is being weakened, not enhanced. What has been created is a closed system, in which neither can supply what the other does not already have. In such a system, there can be survival, but there can be no growth. And where two people are leaning on each other, neither is supporting his or her own weight and, to this extent, is crippled.

Such merging can result from many causes or a combination of causes. It comes from such feelings as, "All we have left now is each other," or "For the first time, my husband really needs me," or "Now that we are together so much more, we're rediscovering each other all over again," or "We're both in the same boat," or "No matter what happens, we know we can rely on each other."

It also comes from a sense of disconnection and mortality —the realization that nothing is forever, that children grow up and leave, that eventually one gives up career, home, neighbors, community, lifelong friends—and ultimately life itself— and that the most important need is for a person, or a relationship, that can be relied upon to *endure*. The unstated pact that emerges is the commitment, no matter what happens, never to separate, each always to be there for the other to cling to in the storm. There is fear—the dread of being alone, of being deserted. There is paralysis—no matter what else changes, we two will always have each other. There is also devotion—each making the other the gift of the remainder of life—and for-giveness—no matter what either of us may say or do, nothing shall sever the tie between us—and concern—whatever may happen to you, I will always be there.

Two people grasping each other so tightly do not support, they smother. In all relationships, some space is necessary across which partners can reach out to each other. People held fast in each other's arms have no freedom to move in any direction or to grasp anything except each other.

The alliance, the relationship of two separately rooted people can be productive for each, but the dependence of two people rooted in each other cannot. Correctly sensing how much dependency, how much leaning upon the other is best, often determines the outcome of the retirement relationship.

For most couples, the sense of being stifled, swallowed up, paralyzed, or smothered acts as an antidote, and there is a kind of rebellion. Frequently, this is enacted as a quarrel in which the husband refuses to watch their scheduled TV program, to go shopping, to play cribbage, or whatever—whatever being some part of their ritual of togetherness. Or it is the wife who says, "For once I'm going to pick out a dress without you—I'm going by myself, and I'll buy what I want" or "If you don't like picking me up at the Book Club, I'll take a cab home—but I'm going anyway. Why don't you find a place of your own to go to?"

Often, the rebellious partner is equally surprised at what is happening—the impulse to rebel seems to come from nowhere and frequently is accompanied by the partner's feeling terribly angry without knowing why. What it is, is a pushing away of the other, and it is often accompanied by all sorts of guilt feelings on one side and a sense of betrayal on the other. There is the underlying panic of "Is even *this* relationship coming apart? Is there no end to what I can lose?"

One woman told me, "I couldn't get my sense of guilt under control, because I did not know whether I was really guilty of anything. I knew Jack was lonely and didn't have anything to do; so I felt guilty about leaving him at home alone when I went off to my discussion group. I even felt guilty about feeling a sense of relief at being out of the house and away from him for a while. I felt guilty about not being able to think of something for him to do instead. Then I told myself that I had a right to go to the meeting by myself and that it was good for me and for him to get away from each other occasionally.

I told myself that finding something to do was his problem, not mine. I tried very hard to convince myself that I alone couldn't be the answer to his loneliness, even if we spent twenty-four hours a day together—that he was lonely for things and people other than me. He would have to find substitutes for them. But it is one thing to tell yourself what is right, and another to feel right."

This kind of ambivalent concern has been expressed to me in many different forms. What it seems to come down to is that each individual adjusts individually. Some require less of an adjustment than others, some take longer adjusting. So both partners rarely proceed to shape their new courses at the same rate of development; one usually is "adjusting" more rapidly than the other, and the difference can sometimes be seen as a subtle form of competition about the relative degree of autonomy they have attained.

"I'm taking the car—I want to get some books at the library."

"Well, if you wait until I've finished practicing, I'll go with you."

"I'd rather go now. I have some other things to do later."

"But I'll be going to the library myself later—why can't you wait so we can go together?"

"I'd rather stick to my own schedule. You could have practiced later, you know."

There are other checkmating moves: Mary agrees to become Secretary of the League of Women Voters, while her husband is co-chairing the Library Fund Drive. She gets a plaque at the end of her term, he gets a scroll.

There are secret messages in this kind of behavior:

"I can get along without you better than you can get along without me."

"I can stand on my own two feet—but you're still leaning on me."

"Other people appreciate me, so you should appreciate me, too."

"I can manage on my own by now; I'm not asking you to help me."

There are quarrels, reconciliations, and compromises. In time, they establish a balance between separateness and togetherness, between dependency and autonomy. It is not just a revision of the social schedule, it is a shifting of the weight of the relationship, so it can be better supported by both. In the process, wounds may be inflicted—recriminations, silences, bitterness, accusations, and much suffering.

But, dismal as it may seem, what is happening is the reassertion of the tension and pull that give a relationship balance and that center its weight.

This struggle may take place unobserved—it all depends on how couples quarrel. Some of the most violent struggles are those occurring on the level of symbols, meta-messages, and covert signals, in the tone of a voice and the way a door is closed, in looking away and in the quality of silence. In other couples, it is as overt as bloody murder. For some it is over fairly quickly, for others it is a form of guerrilla warfare that takes months or years. But it cannot be unresolved forever and is generally past its peak after a couple of years.

Then, usually by odd and devious turns and twists, the couple find themselves going about things differently and to some extent following separate paths in a parallel journey. They may both be attending the same school as before, but now they are taking different courses. Activities which are "his" and those which are "hers" have reemerged. He may study motor repair while his wife takes up weaving—or the other way around. It does not matter which is which; what matters is that they are separate. They no longer read the same books from the library, and he may go to a lecture she has no interest in.

In this arrangement, the man frequently tends toward the activities associated with traditionally male interests, and his wife the female ones. This is not surprising, of course, but it does mark a step back from role reversals. Aside from sports, men tend toward money matters—investment clubs, income tax preparation and advice, fund raising for the Y or civic organizations—while women tend toward community, church, or social causes. The men run the charity car wash, the women the church potluck. The women take responsibility for the appearance of the home, the man for the car.

One man spends the afternoon at the broker's office, watching his investments on the ticker tape while his wife works in the community thrift shop. This enables him to talk at the dinner table about the stock market, and her to talk about the shop. Neither is really an important topic; the entire point is that each has something to tell the other that was not experienced together, so each brings the other something they can share, experiences that provide texture and contrast, that sustain their interest in each other and in their separately unfolding lives.

What all this upheaval and adjustment add up to in the end is one simple lesson that is seemingly very hard to learn: that no one person can be everything to another. Where one has retirement, with its invariable accompaniment, aging, plus relocation, there is so drastic a loss of the structures of support, so drastic a cutting off of the sources of satisfaction, so great a curtailment of psychological nourishment, so great a diminishment of the senses of self-esteem, personal value, and identity, and so widespread a replacement of familiar energizing anxieties by unfamiliar paralyzing anxieties, that it is far beyond the capacity of any single human being, or of any single human relationship, to offset the loss. Where two people, each separately stricken, turn to each other for the things they have formerly gotten elsewhere, they are making impossible demands, and draining each other's emotional energies.

As in the case of two drowning people clinging to each other for survival, the early stages of retirement often consist of the conflict between the need to hold on to the other and the need to loosen the other's stranglehold. The outcome, usually resolved within the first year or two, is the establishment of a different degree of tension, a new balance between holding on and letting go, between dependency and autonomy, between sharing and withholding.

Some never make it out of the crisis period, never achieve the necessary balance. These can be seen in the broken relationships—broken formally by divorce or informally in various degrees of separation. Others seem fortunate to be able to round the dangerous corner without too much stress, often because one partner makes the concessions readily or is completely dominant. Sometimes it is because one secretly prefers the victim role and is more comfortable not being the victor. But the vast majority, it seems to me, work through the scenario to the final compromise, often never fully realizing what is happening to them until it is over and sometimes not even then. One hears such vague descriptions as, "Oh, yes, we had our adjustment problems there for a while, and there were arguments and differences, but we worked them out."

For that matter, despite the lengthy catalogue of retirement problems I have observed, I frequently hear about people who seem immune to and untouched by any of them, whose retirement seems to have gone off without a hitch, who took all obstacles in stride, and who do not understand why anyone else should have difficulty managing what has come so easily to them. I sometimes wonder whether they are more adept at ignoring or suppressing contrary evidence, or are more skillful at making adjustments, or are just more fortunate than the others.

XIX. THREATENING
DEVELOPMENTS

*Threats to tranquil retirement can come from
surprising sources.*

THE FAMILIAR RETIREMENT SCENARIO rarely anticipates correctly the direction from which a potential threat may come. One does not readily think of children or of carefree living as threatening, nor does one expect that the entire retirement plan may have to be scrapped and replaced. In this section, we'll consider all three possibilities.

The adjustment to retirement has been threatened, in more instances than I would have been willing to believe, by a surprising and emotion-laden development: the possibility that after the children have all left the parental home and the couple have reorganized their lives without them, one of the children will want to come home again.

I know the daughter who took off with a group that was deeply involved with drugs and who found a different way of life in another part of the country despite all the family efforts to bring her home. The pain and guilt that parents feel at such a failure never end, but do diminish with time, and eventually they learned to live their life without their daughter. In time the father retired, and the couple made a new life for themselves in the Sun Belt. Shortly after, the daughter telephoned asking if she could come home again.

"There was no way of saying no, and no way of saying yes. We couldn't reject her, nor could we deny her the very thing we had been hoping and praying for. Yet we did not any longer have the home she wanted to return to, and after all we had gone through, the idea of living in the same house with a child we could not understand and facing the strain of helping her through a major adjustment—the demands it made on us for energy, for time, for loving and caring, for financial help, for understanding, all called for things we felt we could no longer give so freely. We felt we might be able to get her straightened out, but at the price of giving up our peace, our stability, our independence, our financial security. We might save her but destroy ourselves."

I was told of the youngest of four children, a handsome teen-ager, who took off one day with a homosexual lover and spent four years on the West Coast, occasionally keeping in touch with his parents. A year after they had been in retirement, he wrote to say that he had broken with his friend and wanted to come home and go into therapy.

The parents telephoned him. "We assured him of our love and our support and told him we would be happy to help him in any way we could. We said good and loving things to each other and made great promises. When we woke up the next morning, we looked at each other, and we both knew immediately we had a huge problem on our hands. The fact is, in the cold light of day, I knew I didn't really mean what I had said and didn't really feel as loving and as unselfish and noble as I had let on. The last thing in the world I wanted was for Jim to come home, to try to live like a family again, to have my new friends meet my son as he was now. And I felt so guilty at feeling that way, and at having lied to Jim about my feelings, about the promises I knew we couldn't keep, about the whole threatening mess, that George and I were the ones who wound up getting therapy."

There were the several divorces, when children who had been joyously married wanted now to go back to the way things were, some of them with infants to be raised by the retired grandparents while their mothers were away at work. There were the college graduates, who had gone into the world to do whatever they considered it their "thing" to do—often despite the advice of their parents—and who had stubbed their toes and wanted to come home, to recuperate, to be restored, so they could sally forth again.

Whatever the particular circumstances, there is a stream of similar scenarios, including one of the child who grows older but does not mature enough to leave home: the full-grown bird still in the nest, refusing to allow the parents to acquit their parental role, draining their reduced retirement income, able to stand only on their shoulders, while unable to become self-sufficient or autonomous.

Except for the last, to which I know no ending that I would describe as happy, the other variations usually turn out to be threats that never materialize. By and large, a child who leaves home knows one can never really return. It is a nice fantasy, and even if attempted briefly it is almost always replaced by some compromise. The drug-scene daughter and the homosexual son, with some financial assistance, worked out a way to live other than with their retired parents. This was also true for many of the divorced children who found it preferable to have the privacy of separate quarters, which made new relationships more feasible.

I am not concerned with the soap opera aspects of these anecdotes, except as they point up forcefully that when the active parental role is ended, which is usually around retirement time, any call to resume it constitutes a major threat to retirement life. In our generation, the underlying assumption in retirement is freedom from the dependence of others on us, and it clearly implies a home without live-in children.

The problem the returning child may pose for parents may be more a factor of relative age than of anything else. Parents who had children late in life or who want early retirement before their children are independent of them necessarily include their parental responsibilities in their retirement plans. But most people put off retirement until their children are out of school and out of the house, married or self-supporting. When they retire, their children are usually young adults, having their first encounters with marriage, with the world after graduation, with complete personal autonomy. They are in a time of youthful risk and experiment; so it is not surprising that, where the experiment fails, it threatens to engulf the parents as well.

Sometimes, the problem of "adjustment" is solved by radically changing its terms. I am a little surprised at the number of second retirements I have encountered; I had thought they were infrequent.

There is the civil servant who retired on an excellent pension and planned to join his brother on the other side of the country and enlarge the brother's private accounting practice by working with him part time. The strain of leaving a post he had held for thirty years, of moving to another locality, and of trying to be effective in a new world of private business proved to be more than he could tolerate, and he had a severe onset of angina.

After his condition stabilized, he found a way to get reinstated to his former position, taking advantage of an obscure technicality. He flourished in the job he had in recent years found to be onerous. To his surprise, he was even promoted —an event he had thought was no longer possible in his career. He spent a couple of years thoroughly enjoying his new responsibilities, earning the recognition and rewards he had long since given up hope of attaining, and then retired again in a great flourish of respect, admiration, and appreciation. He remained in his home city, spending lots of time at his stockbroker's, studying investments, helping friends with tax problems, and finding retirement very pleasant.

I have previously mentioned the high executive of the multinational corporation who, with his excellent retirement benefits, bought a condominium on the fourth hole of one of the best golf courses in the South, where he retired to the envy of his younger associates. Then he discovered that playing golf was not enough. Worse, he saw that his retired neighbors tended to solve their problems by starting to drink at eleven in the morning and by playing cards at all hours. Six months later, he and his wife sold the condominium, moved to a university town, and became deeply involved in the intellectual life of the community.

Neither instance is a good example—people can very rarely tear up a retirement plan and make a new one once they have committed their resources. Most people are trapped in the plan they first make and must learn to make the best of it. But it is good to know that there are those who have been able to afford a second chance and benefit from their first experience. My regret is that retirement today is learned that way, by trial and error, each from his own experience, with very little knowledge of what others have learned from theirs.

In discussions with retired people, when the conversation turns toward any unhappy feelings, there is always someone who will try to turn us away from it as though we were breaking a taboo. "Let's look at the bright side," as though to look away from a feared thing is to make it disappear. It does not make anything disappear—it just represses it, so that the unhappy or fearful person is isolated, quarantined, prevented from sharing his concern with others, examining it and lessening its terror by the light of day, finding ways to deal with it, and perhaps overcoming it.

We unwittingly propagate the myth of perpetually cheerful retirement by failing to examine the implications of the carefree existence. Freedom from care is an attractive prospect. Developers of retirement villages know this very well; it is the key to their success.

It is difficult to find fault with a planned community that offers complete freedom from care. No need to care for the house or the lawn—there is a maintenance crew for that. No need to care about heavy cleaning—there is a cleaning squad that does it. No need to care about transportation—there is a continuous cycle of buses touring the development. No need to care about meals or shopping—there is always a meal available at the commissary. No need to worry about the weather (there are protected walks, sunshine at least 200 days a year), or about health care (a doctor and nurse always on call), or about loneliness (the social director will see to that), or about activity (the craft shop), or improving your mind (concerts and lectures in the social hall).

Like anything carried to an extreme, it creates more problems than it solves, for it forces us to confront the question, "When we are entirely free of our cares, what is left?"

There are no good answers to such a question, for the answer to who you are depends on the answer to "What do you care about?" It is our concerns that shape our identity. When we are stripped of our concerns, we become nothing. To be free of care is to be disconnected.

A young woman told me that she and her husband were concerned about her aged parents, who were living on a small fixed income. "They are very worried about inflation and seem to be very upset at the possibility that they may run out of money. My husband and I assure them that we have enough for all of us, that we will always see that they will never be in want. But no matter how we reassure them, they persist in worrying about it. How can we get them to stop worrying?" It seemed to me that this was a classic illustration.

"Have you considered the possibility that they have a need to worry, to care, to be concerned, and that you should allow them that freedom?" She stared at me.

"Freedom to worry?" she asked.

"I don't know your parents," I responded, "but it seems to me that older people like them may feel more and more separated from the realities of daily life. Their concern about the price of coffee and the increase in electric rates may be not only justified but also their way of maintaining contact, of sharing the same realities that you do. Isn't it possible that what they want to communicate to you is not their fears but something much more wholesome: the message that they are still alive and alert, that they are responsive to what is going on in the world? Expressing a worry about something that might really happen shows a concern about the future rather than a preoccupation with the past. Worrying about a genuine and practical reality like inflation is not indulging in baseless anxiety, it is a way they can become present to you."

I will never know, of course, how close to the mark I was, but it seemed to me there are times people don't want too carefree an existence.

XX. LONELINESS AND THE PROSPECT OF DYING

Men and women are lonely in different ways.
Men are expected to be stronger but to die sooner.

IN ONE WAY OR ANOTHER, the adjustment to retirement must take account of loneliness, a word that is not often used in this context.

When we think of the elderly widow or single woman, we consider loneliness an appropriate word. But this word does not as readily come to mind when we think of the elderly widower or bachelor, and certainly not when we think of the retired husband.

Only in recent years have I realized that men are lonely and that in some ways their loneliness is different from the loneliness of women. I have begun to suspect that men may also be lonelier than women. And finally, I believe that many men are unconscious of their loneliness and are startled if they become aware of it.

I tend to see women as coming close to other women far more easily, readily, and often than men approach other men. I suggest there is a sisterhood among women, but there is not really a brotherhood among men. One reason may be that women talk freely with one another about what they feel; men talk to and at one another about what they think. I do not intend to speculate on the reasons for this, but I tend to notice the difference everywhere and in small things as well as large. Do men talk about feelings at all? Of course they do—but mostly with women. John Leonard has written in *The New York Times*, "This is the way it usually works with men: we meet in the infantry trench or the locker room or the box seat or the saloon. We talk about politics, money, sports, sex, and other abstractions. (My impression is that these days we aren't talking as much about sex as we used to, but I am often wrong.) We seldom talk about our children unless they are triumphant or cute, and if we ever talk about ourselves, we will probably lie; to admit to an existential funk would be unmanly. Inside the abstractions, however, we are warm and safe. . . . When men—at least the men I know in this country—require a . . . true friend, we usually look to a woman. Secretly, men do not feel that we are very interesting people. That a woman should occasionally find us fascinating comes as a surprise, a gratifying gift. Whereupon we impart so many griefs, joys, fears, hopes, suspicions, counsels and oppressions of the heart that our women, on the whole, would prefer to watch television. Thus, over and over again, we learn that we have much to be modest about. . . .

"According to La Rochefoucauld, 'What men have given the name of friendship to is nothing but an alliance, a reciprocal accommodation of interest, an exchange of good offices; in fact it is nothing but a system of traffic, in which self-love always proposes to itself some advantage.' La Rochefoucauld, as usual, was wrong. Men seek in friendship a demilitarized zone."

However it may come about, men make business friendships with other men; women make personal ones. So the mechanism for men to form new friendships is limited largely to the business world. The competition of that world requires that friendships must be useful or mutually advantageous.

Where there is also a reciprocated regard or mutual respect, the business relationship often expands to become somewhat personal—in the sense that two men might meet for lunch even if they have no business to transact. Even so, their conversation will tend largely to shop talk.

The relationship might widen further to include their wives, meeting at each other's homes, on the golf course, or at the country club. Such relationships have every appearance of being truly personal, but their special character is revealed when either man has a job change. The man who gets a new job generally leaves his "friends" behind, maintaining links only with those who may continue to be useful. When he goes into retirement, therefore, he takes few or no friends with him.

In retirement, he no longer has associates, opposite numbers in other companies, superiors and subordinates, who formed the pool of people with whom friendships were possible. His only basis for meeting other men and forming relationships with them dwindles to such things as sports, hobbies, and volunteer activities, superficial links that lead to superficial relationships.

There are women, usually his wife, to whom he can express his feelings, but he no longer knows, at this stage of his life, what his feelings are. So when he speaks of loneliness, if he does, both of them may think he is expressing a need for female companionship or a social relationship with other couples. Neither is aware that he is actually lonely for other men, that he longs for contact with his own species, the kind of sharing that has nothing to do with sex but rather with common denominators of life experience. To say it another way, he needs other men with whom he can find the relief of finally lowering his guard, of entering what John Leonard called the demilitarized zone.

In later years, and certainly in retirement, he becomes aware that he is inhabiting a different kind of society from the one he has known. He is not only lonely, he has become a minority.

This kind of loneliness cannot really be shared with women. Many men, not knowing what it is they are feeling, tend to isolate themselves by following some solitary routine, puttering, or repairing, or losing themselves in some meaningless obsession such as watching sports on television or writing letters to the newspapers about tax reform. Some of them die of this lack of intimacy without ever knowing why or having been aware that they were suffering at all, which may in some small way account for part of the difference in the life expectancies of men and women.

This difference in life expectancy is an awareness most of us carry throughout our lives, but for the greater part of that time it has only an intellectual or abstract meaning that tells us what we already know: Some people live longer than others.

When we cross the sixties, heading for the seventies, it acquires sudden new significance, for inevitably a man's thinking about retirement must consider how long a time he must provide for, not only for himself but also for his wife. This, too, is the time of life when he begins to lose friends to cancer, stroke, or heart attack. He also begins to be aware of something he might have expected but didn't actually foresee—the increasing number of widows in his peer group. Many of the wives he meets are in their second marriages, and conversations more frequently include references to "my first husband." One becomes more concerned with wills and estates. And all these influences converge to form an implicit assumption: In marriage, the man will die and the woman will survive him. This is made explicit by courses in investment management for women, so they can manage the estates left them by their husbands, and by all the other things, from plumbing to car repair, women are now being encouraged to study. It is

166

expected of a "good" husband that he will look ahead and provide for his wife's needs even after he has passed away. All these things combine to produce a heightened sense of mortality in a man and so, on a deeper level, a sense of being the weaker. But he is expected to act like the stronger of the two, to teach her how to take over his tasks and responsibilities when he dies and to continue to provide for her financial security, even after he is dead.

It is not my intention to discuss the implications of such a relationship. Important as it is, it is irrelevant to my purpose. I want to call attention to the dissonance between these two expectations and the emotional cross-currents they must create. Underlying all this there is another dimly recognized process that echoes retirement: the transfer of power, the sense of handing over to another, of leaving behind what others will continue.

I have heard little or no comment from men or women about the remarkable fact that one of them is foredoomed. It is stated as a fact, but not commented upon. I find it hard to accept, and in my own case I can refute the idea that this fact has no emotional content. I feel a deep resentment that because I am a man my life-span is shortened by eight or nine years. This seems arbitrary and punitive, and I don't know what I did to deserve this penalty. I would expect an uproar over it, but there isn't. I would think there would be nothing more urgent on the feminine agenda than to find a remedy, an answer to the question of "Why do our husbands die so much earlier than we do?"

Rather, there seems to be a resigned acceptance, indeed a sort of self-pity evidenced by some women, that considers the husband's death to be the final burden inflicted upon her, for it is he who makes her a widow. I cannot believe I am alone in these feelings, but I must confess that I have not found many others who will admit to sharing them. This may be one of the more deeply secretive of the emotions I have been discussing.

Another consideration involving age acquires new meaning at the onset of the retirement years; it is the traditional age differential between husbands and wives. I have remarked about this in terms of planning a time to retire, pointing out that the husband generally reaches retirement age before his wife does, and some of the problems that follow. As we progress into the retirement years, this differential shows another aspect, this time related to things more substantial than a retirement timetable.

We generally think of a husband as two or three years older than his wife. This is an average; there are many marriages in which the difference is greater. The greater disparity is perhaps more frequent in later-life second marriages; divorced older men often marry women several years younger than their first wives. But in any case most men go into retirement as people older than their wives, and this creates a confluence of problems, one stream flowing from retirement, the other from aging.

An age difference of five years or so makes very little difference when the parties are in their forties or fifties. But once into their sixties the difference acquires enormous significance because it is paired with earlier fatality. The man will not only die at an age eight or nine years younger than his wife; he is already four or five years nearer to the end. It is the sum of the two that intensifies the difference.

This cannot help but have an effect on their concepts of each other and of themselves. Again we find the disheartening effect; he finds it necessary to resist other people's expectations of him, as well as his expectations of himself. What is expected of him is *decline*; to avert it he must struggle to retain his health, his capacity for achievement, his self-esteem, to yield ground very slowly, if at all. What has already begun to die is any expectation that he will gain ground, make progress, *improve*. What is being erased is his potential.

The opposite is true of his younger wife, who assumes, consciously or unconsciously, that she will someday be widowed. For her, all the dynamics work in the direction of increasing her personal strength, not only because she may begin to take over more and more of the management of their affairs, but also because she knows there is much she must learn to prepare herself for survival. There is an implicit assumption that if she will invest the energy she can become stronger, and more self-reliant. What is being assumed is her potential for growth and improvement.

In retirement, one sees on every hand the protected husband and the more vigorous wife. He has his nap or his medication, he is excused from lifting or anything else physically arduous. He is also excused from little gallantries that might be taxing, such as standing when there aren't enough seats, getting the car from the parking lot when it is raining, holding open the door in the drafty hallway. He leaves the concert at intermission; he takes the lighter bag at the checkout counter. His wife does more of the driving. To some observers they may seem to be acting out a self-fulfilling prophecy.

XXI. RETIRING AS SEPARATE
FROM AGING

*If a person thinks of retirement as entering old age,
he draws all sorts of erroneous conclusions about
what is happening to him.*

WE BEGAN DISCUSSING retirement, but now we seem to be talking about aging. It is difficult to avoid doing that and hard to draw a clear line between the two.

There are retired people who do not feel old, and old people who never retire, but people tend to think about "getting older" around the same time they begin to think about retiring. Unless they are careful, they tend to think of the two as being one, of the process of becoming a retired person as being the same as the process of becoming an old person.

If a person thinks of retirement as entering old age, he draws all sorts of erroneous conclusions about what is happening to him. He attributes some of the temporary adjustments of retirement to the permanent onset of old age and creates a self-fulfilling prophecy in which he confirms his identity as an old person.

He considers time to be his enemy and does not realize that to anyone adjusting to retirement time is an ally. He confuses his disconnection with the business world with withdrawal from meaningful activity, his loss of his executive functions with the loss of his physical abilities, his lowered productivity with his "uselessness" as an old man. He limits his ability to grow by believing he is in a state of decline. He is unable to see the future as having possibilities because he sees it instead as the downward path to the grave. *There is no way he can become a new person if he is convinced he is an old person.*

We tend to confuse retirement with aging because by the time we retire we are living in a peer group of older people, and we spend most of our time in their company. We begin to attribute all the characteristics of these people, and of ourselves, to age.

This is what Korzybski called elementalism, the habit of explaining complex things as resulting from single causes (whatever older people do, they do because they are old) and of reducing people to a single characteristic (older people are only old, they are nothing else).

When we were younger, we were part of a younger peer group; we knew that we forgot things and misplaced them, had pains and illnesses, wore glasses or had hearing problems, but we considered these things to be part of everyday life, not indications of how old we were. But now we feel surrounded by people who do not see so well, hear so well, are less vigorous, have more aches and pains, take more medication. They constantly remind us they "aren't getting any younger," and they serve unconsciously as role models whose mannerisms we adopt simply because people tend to conform to their peers.

When we can't remember a telephone number, we say, "I'm getting old—my memory isn't so good anymore." Thirty years earlier, when we could not remember a phone number we might have said, "I'm a scatterbrain—I should write these things down." We would not have attributed our lapse to aging, although we were aging a year at a time, every year, even way back then.

When we were in our twenties and had shoulder pains after a day of flycasting, we said we had a "charley-horse." Today we tend to say, "I'm getting too old for this kind of thing; the old joints aren't what they used to be."

These are self-inflicted wounds, acts of cruelty we perpetrate on ourselves by attributing everything we deplore about ourselves to our age. We are far less tolerant of ourselves than others are of us, and we seem intent on teaching the young to see us only as being old and to see being old as being handicapped. People who have worn glasses since childhood will say, "Wait just a minute while I put on my glasses; I don't see as good as I used to anymore."

Perhaps we don't spend as much time as we should among younger people. If we did, it might help us remember how many of them have aches and pains, bruises and bandages, casts and crutches, physical handicaps of all kinds, how often they are sick, require surgery, or need medical care—and all this without ever a thought or word about getting older. But as we move into our sixties we begin to load all these and more onto a single cause—aging, as though young people are not arthritic and asthmatic, do not have heart trouble, never forget names, and never misplace things.

When the vague and general anxieties of retirement begin to plague us, "getting old" provides the handiest focus for them. We attribute our fearfulness, our sense of loss, all our latent uneasiness to the fact that we are getting old. And this is reinforced by the resemblance I have previously mentioned between retirement and death. The latent fears of retirement and those of aging are the same: death, poverty, sickness, loneliness, rejection, uselessness, powerlessness.

Summed up this way, they seem too much to overcome. But, like most of the things we fear, all of these things do not come to all of us. Far more people fear poverty in retirement than actually become impoverished; we live in fear of sickness far longer than we actually experience it; and the feelings of loneliness, rejection, uselessness, and powerlessness are almost always those we have generated in ourselves and can overcome if we can believe there is a future for us.

We all spend our lives in the valley of the shadow of death, and some of us waste our lives fearing it. Others live more usefully because of it. Others simply do not dwell on it. But death is no more frightening to the old than to the young. Indeed, the young tend to fear it more, for time helps to diminish some of its awesome mystery. But that is another subject.

What seems important to learn is how to separate becoming a retired person from becoming an old person. It is important to recognize that retirement comes on a given day while the coming of age is not only slower, it is much less well defined, and it is relative. We know that we *grow older*; we don't know when we *become old*. I think it may be said that we become old when we declare ourselves to be old—and that is why I think it is so important to stop speaking prematurely of ourselves as old.

When a man is able to make the separation, to look at retirement as a condition separate from aging, he can see some of the facts that have been obscured.

He can see that we have added to our life cycle a new stage, a time of still considerable vitality, interposed between our working life and our old age—not, as we tend to think, additional years of decrepitude tacked on at the end of our lives to prolong the terminal period. More important, he can see that we have not yet developed a function for this new life-stage, that the retired do not yet serve a recognizably useful social purpose.

The current generation of retirees are the pioneers in this

new life cycle, and they constitute a new social class.

When future social scientists look back at us, they will see clearly what we have only begun to recognize—that with our generation there has come into being a new form of leisure class—a leisure class of moderate means. We have long known the idle rich and the idle poor; what is new is the idle middle class.

Their primary characteristic is that they consume but they do not produce. They have incomes for which they do no work. They have ten or twenty or more years of potentially productive life, but no clearly formulated sense of the purpose of these years. They are a generation whose only established relationship to the rest of society, as yet, is to constitute a market for what others produce, to serve as consumers in our consumer society.

We need more than this to justify our existence. We must consciously try to invent a future, to find purposes and goals appropriate to this new stage of life, to develop life-styles that best fit it, and to make it separate and distinct from aging.

The aged are developing militancy. There is a growing awareness of "gray power," of "Senior Citizens" as a voting bloc fighting for special benefits in taxation, housing, medical care, and social services. Whatever the merits or demerits of the causes of the elderly, they are different from the causes of the retired. They are not mutually exclusive and can well be fought concurrently. But they are not the same.

The causes of the elderly may be security, care, or equality. The cause of the retired is one of function. What I would like to hear, and don't hear, is widespread discussion of the question, "What are retired people good for?" This is the question every retired person has to answer for himself. Until better answers are found, capable and useful people will try to lead stereotypical existences that make no demands on their intellect and no use of their life experience, in that mythical retirement world in which there is no loneliness, worry, sickness, and death; in short, a time and place devoid of meaning. Those who look behind the myths and stereotypes see retired couples who drift apart psychologically and emotionally, whose children and grandchildren comprise their only remaining bond except for a common financial arrangement. Or we see couples who turn so fiercely to each other for satisfactions neither can provide that they live in outright hostility or, if they can afford separate lives, go on alone. We see couples where the sickness of either becomes the intolerable burden on the other, and where the death of one is the blow from which the other never fully recovers. We see aging couples increasingly isolated in deteriorating neighborhoods, with steadily fewer friends and relatives, and trapped by an inability to devise alternatives. We see men dying of ailments, sudden or chronic, whose medical diagnoses conceal the fact that they really die of loneliness, of uselessness, of life emptiness, in despair of finding their way back to affirmation of their own worth, understanding only dimly if at all why they are unable to overcome their soul sickness. We read of the rising suicide rate of the elderly, particularly of men. And through it all, we strive not to speak or think of these aspects of retirement, obeying the sickroom code of avoiding the unpleasant, looking at the bright side, not upsetting the patient.

This false optimism prevents us from finding ways of making retirement more *manageable,* less of a wounding experience, a culmination worthy of the lifetime of striving that precedes it.

It prevents us from exploring such important questions as, "Is retirement good for people?" and "Is the retirement of their people good for the companies they retire from?"

Obviously, retirement may be good for some people but not for everyone. There are those to whom retirement is a solution and not a problem, who, despite all I have recounted, have only a happy experience with it and so do not require our concern here. But to force some people into retirement might be, like capital punishment, "cruel and unusual"; for others, the stress of retirement might be, like smoking, "dangerous to your health." Now that we have reached the time when retirement is becoming the normal way to end a business career, it is appropriate to ask whether it is the desired or desirable end for everyone; I believe that for those who would be more hurt than helped by it, there should be alternatives.

We may be able to think of new ways some people can remain in their careers or professions if they prefer. Besides inventing the new retired class, we might also try to invent a new kind of working class, people who have the security and freedom of retirement but who continue to function in the working world, who may have no authority but who still retain considerable influence.

We may conclude that life wisdom is too valuable an asset to be automatically discarded. Perhaps elders can play a useful role in a business organization especially because they are above the battle and no longer compete with anyone. With no self-interest at risk, they may provide the missing ingredient in the makeup of management: neutrality. Unlike the people still pursuing their careers and personal goals, they can, perhaps, be more objective, disinterested, nonpolitical, fairer.

Possibly they can see the future more clearly and with less distortion because it is a place they are helping to prepare not for themselves but for others. And, because they can also see farther into the past, perhaps they can think in a larger conceptual framework.

Companies may, if they look, find ways their older employees need not be expelled but can instead be used as advisors, consultants, developers of their business philosophy, definers of their social responsibilities, guardians of their long-range goals, conciliators and mediators in their internal disputes, historians, reporters, speakers of the necessary but unpopular points of view, the politically unwise but sensible minority opinions.

It seems to me worthwhile to investigate converting the English political idea of a "shadow government" to the administrative concept of a "shadow management" of employees-out-of-office, a second team, who can give ideas, proposals, plans, or budgets a first runthrough, a tryout or rehearsal, a pilot test, or a final polish.

In short, when we know more about present-day retirement and can bring ourselves to look at some of its wounds, we may decide we are going about it incorrectly, that it is not right for some people, who should be given alternatives, and that it is a waste of talent for some companies, which should be using what they now discard.

For those who do retire, if we know how and when the greatest stresses are likeliest to occur, we can to some extent find ways to diminish them. If we recognize that it is the suddenness and totality of retirement that make it so hard to adjust to, we can explore ways of entering it gradually, and of having trial and rehearsal periods that will make it easier to take.

We may find ways to gain time in which to restore a sense of identity or to define one's altered identity in an acceptable way.

We may avoid the impact of having to make all our adjustments at once, and the possible mistake of relocating at the same time as we retire.

We may find ways men can get in touch with their feelings and get emotional support from other men, can avoid the isolation of feeling stranded in a feminine world, perhaps in men's support groups equivalent to those women have developed in the last decade.

It may be possible to find ways in which couples can prepare to withstand the strains on their marriage, knowing that both are about to enter a period of adjustment, not only to retirement but also to each other.

Perhaps knowing what retirement feels like may enable us far earlier in life to find an answer to what is meaningful to us when we no longer have our work to give us meaning.

A retired executive who had found meaning in his career only after he began to work assumed he would similarly find some satisfying purpose in his retirement when he stopped working. When this did not happen, he was furious.

"I have spent almost fifty years educating myself, improving myself, learning my skills, polishing my judgment, advancing my career, managing my money, doing my work, always getting better or trying to. All to what purpose? To putter in the garden, to pitch horseshoes, to play golf? I can't believe that my fifty years of preparation can culminate in such trivial goals. There must be a purpose important enough to justify what I invested to get to this point. I refuse to believe I climbed the mountain just to sit on a park bench."

But a man must decide while climbing the mountain what he wants to find at the top; it is too late to start thinking about it when he gets there. We must be able to stop spending most of our working years reaching our career goals without ever giving a thought to the goals we will want to reach after our careers are ended.

XXII WHY HOBBIES
ARE NOT ENOUGH

*Why a hobby cannot be a satisfactory substitute for
an occupation. Some criteria for satisfying
retirement activities.*

How can the executive minimize some of the adverse
effects of loss of power, of lowered self-esteem, of isolation
after retirement?

The conventional wisdom, which I do not deprecate, is
that in the years preceding retirement he should develop outside interests, activities, and hobbies. I have already commented on the fact that these almost always seem, to a
successful operating executive, to be childish, trivial, and
unsatisfying. It may help them find better alternatives if we
consider why a hobby cannot be a satisfactory substitute for
an occupation: It simply does not generate the same kinds of
psychic satisfaction. Hobbies may entertain or amuse us, interest and occupy us, but they rarely make the adrenalin flow
the way winning a budget battle does. In our outside interests,
we generally have nothing at risk, as we do in our careers.

I tend to think the answer is almost self-evident. The
preretiring executive certainly should develop outside interests
and activities, but if they are to replace some of the emotional
supports that fall away at retirement, they must be designed

179

to approximate and embrace similar kinds of tension, high level of difficulty, possibility of failure, and covert competition that we have become addicted to in our business lives, that kick off the conditioned responses in us that keep us feeling alive and worthwhile.

Crafts, such as woodworking or gem-polishing, simply cannot do this for us. One man I know found his answer in designing his retirement home and building it in his preretirement years. It was not merely a matter of sketching a room plan for a contractor to develop; he began by studying site selection and site location—how to select the land on which to build and how to place the structure on the site. He checked his critical decisions with a licensed architect at each crucial point, but the decisions were his. He studied and read up on structural design and space utilization and proceeded step by step through every stage of home design, selection of materials, and construction techniques, until he was ready to begin construction. Then he hired a builder with whom he worked out an arrangement for "sweat equity," that is, for him to participate in the actual work of construction, doing assigned parts of the job, in return for a corresponding reduction in the labor cost.

"It was expensive. Afterward, I realized many ways in which I had incurred unnecessary costs. It was slow; the entire project moved ahead only as fast as I was able to keep up with it, and when the actual construction began there were periods when we just stopped work because I was not available. It was inefficient; as I learned, I kept going back and changing things already done, and the architect was not always free to look over my shoulder when I wanted him to.

"On the other hand, I really had no immediate need for the house—my retirement was four years away. Part of what money I lost by inefficiency I gained by doing so much of the work myself. And I did end up with a home I felt was truly mine, more than just financially. It was exactly the way I wanted it. I felt I knew every nail hole, and there was nothing about the piping or the wiring or the heating system that I didn't understand and couldn't fix. When I started, I didn't even know how door chimes worked."

If we look more closely at what happened here, we can see several things that suggest a good general direction. First, the task provided a genuine sense of achievement. More important, the achievement was not a private one, performed in the solitude of a basement workshop; it was public and visible. Many of us are so other-oriented that not only must we ourselves approve of what we do, but it seems essential for our self-esteem that we also have the approbation of others—recognition of our worth.

Second, it was a real-life task, unlike making a decorative plaque or another coffee table; it produced an actual home, and its value was recognizable to a banker.

Third, it enabled using authority—over the architect, the builder, the suppliers, and all the other people involved in the project, for our executive was undoubtedly the project boss and he made the major decisions. Further, it involved him deeply with a large number of other people whom he would otherwise never have met: the teachers of the courses he took and the other students, the people he encountered in his library research, those he sought out for help and advice and for specialized knowledge and skills, large numbers of casual acquaintances at the lumber yard, building supply houses, survey office, and other places where people involved in home building tend to congregate and give one another a hand; the local tradespeople and town officials in his new location, and a great many potential neighbors, near and far, who came by and stopped to chat because they were curious about him. Indeed, "the fellow who's putting up that house on Blue Ridge" became a fairly well-known figure in the community before he ever moved down permanently, because the project ran on for a little more than two years.

Finally, the entire project was something of a risk, venturing as it did into his areas of ignorance; he was making judgments without experience and backing them with money on which there might be no return. That gave it the bitter tang of reality that took it out of the class of things we think of as hobbies or interests.

"But that's not really all there is to it," he told me. "It did a great deal to the way I felt about things. For one thing, it made me feel a sense of anticipation about retiring—it meant I would be free to move permanently into this new home I came to love so well. It made me feel comfortable in the community; I knew I was not going to a place where I would be a stranger when I arrived. It also gave me a very strong personal focus on something that was entirely unrelated to my work and my career [he was a systems and procedures analyst for a communications company] and reassured me that I could give up all of that without being too badly hurt by the loss—I knew I could get my satisfactions elsewhere. Perhaps most important, it kept me thinking about myself as a retired person at some future time, so I began to evolve a clear picture of the kind of life I would lead and how I would go about things; I had some long and fruitful daydreams while pounding nails into the roof shingles. When the time came, it was all familiar and welcome to me, and I didn't spend much time looking back."

In this one activity he had, perhaps unwittingly, incorporated antidotes to most of the psychological losses retirement could bring: loss of power, self-esteem, recognition, and achievement. It had provided the beginning of new links to other people and the community at large, pathways to new relationships (especially relationships with other men) that averted a growing sense of isolation. And it had helped wean him away from his preoccupation with his job, turned his mind toward more clearly contemplating his future, and provided a transition to a new life-style.

The building of this retirement house was a deeply gratifying experience to this man, obviously—so gratifying that he was unwilling to stop. After he retired, he built a summer cottage at the other end of the state and, without planning it, became involved in other projects. At one time, he bought a tract of land and built a few houses of his own design on it and sold them. He helped several friends in the design and building of their homes. He never really became a builder, an architect, a designer, a contractor, a consultant, a real estate broker, or an appraiser, but he was always busy with some aspect of construction. When I met him, he was already widely regarded as a man who "knew everything" about passive solar heating.

For him the transition into retirement was comparatively easy, because his choice of outside interests before retirement answered the question I posed at the beginning of this chapter.

It illustrates, too, some of my comments about investing. He had made a financial "investment" by building a house more expensively, more inefficiently, than he might otherwise have done. He invested his time—large amounts of it—and his physical labor as well as considerable mental energy. He may have thought he was investing these things in a home; he was really investing them in making the retirement transition successfully.

This choice example, fortunately, illustrates almost everything I want to say about how to select appropriate outside interests and "hobbies" prior to retirement, but I do not mean that everyone should follow this example.

I know a retired dentist who achieved many of the same things by an entirely different course. Concerned with social issues, he had long been involved in advocacy organizations such as the American Civil Liberties Union and community organizations such as the United Fund. In the community to which he retired, he helped organize a dispute settlement center to help mediate differences outside the courtroom and took some intensive training in mediation. With this training, for the challenge, he took an examination for appointment as a federal mediator, work that was intermittent but required him to be available when called on. Somewhat to his surprise, he received the appointment. Examined closely, one is able to see that in this work he was able to get satisfactions equivalent to those our house builder found in his: self-esteem, recognition, and replenishment for loss of power and authority. And, being in the midst of other people's conflicts, he could never feel isolated.

A friend took another course: Starting as a volunteer worker, he rose through the ranks of RSVP (Retired Senior Volunteer Program) until he was appointed to the regional board of directors. At this administrative and policy-making level, most of his psychic needs are satisfied. He did not begin to move toward this outcome until after he had retired, however; so he did have a period of almost two years during which the adjustment was difficult.

Not all these ventures work out happily. I have in mind an advertising executive who determined to retire at sixty and spend his remaining years doing something he had always wanted to do. Strangely enough, it was to become a dental technician—a choice that illustrates how individual and unique people can be. What he did was to start at the very beginning and take the full course of study that would qualify him in his occupation; it took almost two years, which he considered to be his investment in his new retirement career.

Then he applied to every dentist and dental laboratory in the area, only to learn that they were suspicious of a sixty-two-year-old man who had retired from advertising to become a dental technician; there was something in these circumstances that, no matter how he explained them, caused uneasiness.

He did not succeed in getting anyone to hire him, and when I last saw him he was pondering alternatives. I mention this instance to counteract any tendency to believe that all retirement plans, no matter how unusual, will succeed if one spends enough energy and enthusiasm on them. However, it is this very hazard, this lack of certainty, that provides a necessary element of risk, such as we have in our working careers and in our satisfying retirement activities, but not in our hobbies.

XXIII. NEGOTIATING
THE TRANSITION

Some suggested strategies for negotiating the circumstances under which you will retire.

ARE THERE WAYS TO MAKE the experience of retirement less traumatic, to make the transition into retirement easier? My desk is piled high with answers others have proposed; yet I have not been able to find an answer that seems appropriate and responsive *to me*. Like most of the literature on retirement, these books, articles, and pamphlets repeat one another endlessly. All of them echo the single most insistent message: *The key to successful retirement is advance planning.* This is undeniably true. But the recommended planning seems to consist of completing an endless array of checklists and questionnaires, dividing and subdividing the process into the tiniest particles. The reader is asked to respond yes-or-no to such statements as "I'm keeping up with events so that I shall not come to be regarded as a 'has-been' " and "I see to it that I get enough rest every day."

Philip Slater, commenting on the fact that in books of this kind the writer is supposed to offer concrete suggestions for some sort of action, says, "The recommendations that are made always seem fatuous to me—either so vague and general as to be implicit in the analysis itself, or so concrete and trivial

186

that one could have offered them without going through any of the analysis."

I have before me a pamphlet entitled *"What I Wish Someone Had Told Me About Retirement—"* The Realities of Retirement as Seen by 50 American Men and Women. The well-meant advice consists of such things as getting a thorough medical checkup, developing new interests while working, not hanging on to your job too long after you reach sixty-five, not visiting the old office too frequently, and making dining out with friends a "Dutch treat." The preponderant message, however phrased, is: Plan and prepare well in advance. Beyond this sound advice, it seems to me that the "reality" reported by these fifty American men and women is either too trivial or too general, and I am not convinced that a reasonably intelligent person would be persuaded by it significantly to change his behavior.

Woodrow W. Hunter, of the University of Michigan, has written a highly respected book, *Preparation for Retirement*, that consists of very careful, detailed instructions, each segment ending with a list of "Questions to Think About" ("Why is it that some older people are lonely?") and each section ending with a checklist on "Retirement Readiness." He concludes with a small collection of "Short Stories," anecdotes describing various experiences of retired people, to stimulate thinking and facilitate discussion with other people planning to retire. I certainly have no quarrel with his concepts of planning, thinking, and discussing, for all of which Mr. Hunter has provided an excellent framework, but to me this textbook method is too stilted and pedantic; it stifles my ability to think creatively and imaginatively.

Also in the pile on my desk is an article in the *Harvard Business Review*, with the provocative title "Can You Survive Your Retirement?" written by Leland P. Bradford, who reports many of the kinds of distress I have commented on, and describes some of the marital difficulties and societal attitudes that produced them. However, his concluding section, "What Can Be Done," speaks of only one thing— corporate preretirement counseling programs. He concludes by briefly laying the final responsibility on the retiree and his "will and initiative to seek new activities and socialization patterns."

On the other hand, Elmer Otte, another respected writer in the field, believes that retirement, as the subtitle of his *Guidebook* says, is a "task you must do for yourself." For this task, Mr. Otte offers the *Retirement Rehearsal Guidebook*, containing "Helpful Planning Exercises" constituting, in Mr. Otte's intention, a "rehearsal" of the actual retirement. This means filling out charts and checklists, and answering page after page of questions, and using maps, tax tables, cost of living and climatological data to pin oneself down to specific decisions. It has timetables and frequent "Progress Report to Myself" checklists. It also has lists of things, lists I find personally dismaying, but which may have value for the readers Mr. Otte has in mind: "Some Ways to Add to Retirement Income" includes such items as "winning prizes," "earthworm growing," "painting trays," and (can he be serious?) "hare raising." The "Personal and family resources" checklist, which is a reminder of "How abundant your resources really are," includes "Compassion," "Political interest," "Churchwork wishes," "Golfer's low handicap," "outgoing love," and "interest in most anything."

Between the alternatives of offering general principles which are already apparent and are widely offered elsewhere, or specific and concrete directives which could not possibly be appropriate to each individual, I shall try to steer a new course: to make a few proposals that everyone might consider, although fewer could follow, but which have either not been offered elsewhere to my knowledge or which are not widely known. These deal with action, things that might be done. I shall also offer some points of view, a few angles of vision that might give insight, a different way, perhaps, of looking at the same thing. These deal with attitudes. I cannot tell you what to feel, what to think, or what to do. But I can suggest some possible behaviors and some possible ways of thinking about them.

I have mentioned the reluctance of the working executive to think about retirement and his consequent failure to prepare for it. No amount of advice about what he should think about and how he should prepare for it will do any good unless a way can be found to capture his attention. What I will try to do is to make the kinds of suggestions such an executive would respond to because they may show him how he can use his current powers and skills to his own better advantage and how to become a little better *at the game he is already playing.*

It seems unarguable that the severity of the retirement trauma is generally related to the suddenness of the transition; the more changes and adaptations one is required to make simultaneously, the greater the stress and distress. So the common-sense remedy would seem to be to find ways to enter retirement gradually or partially. The people I know who have had the fewest problems are usually those who only partially retired before they stopped working altogether. But there is an important distinction to be made. It is between retiring and *then* going into some part-time occupation —all the activities the books suggest to supplement retirement income—and not fully retiring in the first place.

There is great value in a transition period during which one has not fully lost all ties to one's career and the people associated with it. This is different from cutting those ties and then trying to make new ones.

What deserves careful exploration is the possibility of continuing to perform some function, however reduced, in the environment in which one already has know-how and sure-footedness. One too obvious direction is in consulting work, drawing on one's experience and knowledge while it is still up to date. Another is in project work: some task-force assignment that has a well-defined ending point and that would require taking someone else away from his regular work if you were not available. I have discussed this possibility with others and have met the usual catalogue of negative responses:

"That wouldn't work for me—my company just doesn't hire consultants, and if they do they prefer to go to some prestigious consulting firm."

"They'd always give an assignment like that to one of the younger men."

"We just don't have need for consultants, and I don't know any projects they could assign me to."

These are valid objections, and they tend to account for the fact that most men who retire do so without any transition period. But the need for such a transition makes it worthwhile to take another look at the problem and dig a little deeper for a solution.

"Suppose you had five years to work up the kind of project you could handle—do you think you could work things out so that a project of this sort would be coming to a head just about the time you became available to handle it? In five years, could you plant enough seeds, do enough quiet missionary work, get enough consensus, so that the assignment would be waiting for you by the time you got to it?"

When I have asked such a question of a successful operating executive, I could almost always see his mental wheels begin to spin, as he calculated the political strategy that would be required and weighed the chances he could pull it off.

Many men don't think this way simply because they are not thinking about the need for the transition period five years ahead; when and if they begin to recognize it, it is often too late to accomplish what must be done. But, planned well in advance as part of a personal retirement strategy, it is sometimes a well-conceived solution.

There is no way I can specify the answer for each individual, but a few examples may help spur the imagination.

One man, faced with the decision of his company to give a consulting assignment to an outside firm, did a good job of persuading the executive who had awarded the contract that the award should stipulate that the consulting company employ him to work on the project on a part-time basis. This was not a boondoggle; he could provide important company insights to the consulting firm and also serve his employer by monitoring the job for which they were paying such high fees. But both companies knew that, after a stipulated time when the job had been done, he would be out of their hair. It was a case of everybody wins, nobody loses.

Another man was a sales manager at corporate headquarters in New York City. His plan was to retire to a condominium in Florida. Rather than wait until his retirement, he negotiated a special arrangement: to groom his assistant to take over his job two years before he was scheduled to retire, then to step down and take over management of the Southeast region, which included Florida, for his last two years.

"During that last two-year period I was the company's anchor man and insurance policy. I was the strongest manager in the field, and I not only built up the region, but I also set a faster pace for all the other regional managers to follow. Meanwhile, I was grooming a local manager to take over the region from me when I retired. And finally, the company had my assurance that if the man I had trained in New York to succeed me in the national job didn't work out, I was still available to fill the breech.

"But meanwhile, I was accomplishing several things for myself. First, I was getting myself and my family settled in Florida, putting down roots, and getting the feel of the place as a home. Second, as the end of the final year approached, I turned more and more of the job over to my successor and began spending increasing amounts of time at home with my wife, making friends, developing alternative activities and interests. Finally, due to my reduced income—I took a salary cut when I accepted the regional job—I got a good bearing on my financial situation in retirement, knew just how my overhead would run, and could assure myself that my retirement income was sufficient to support my style of living."

These are highly individual experiences, of course, but that is exactly the important point: that in almost every working executive's situation, there is the potential for some special arrangement whereby the interests of his company and his own retirement strategy could be made to coincide, particularly if the executive has his objective in mind several years ahead.

It is not always a matter of manipulating events so as to conform to the strategic objective; it is also a matter of being alert to developments which could move in that direction and could be utilized for strategic purposes.

I have begun to use the word "strategy" in the last few sentences because I want to suggest the appropriate state of mind: that of being faced with a task for which various strategies can be devised. This is far better than the attitude of facing an event that, if it cannot be averted, must then be endured.

The greatest asset of the successful executive is his ability to devise strategies for specific ends and his deftness and skill in enacting these strategies in an environment of competitive power politics—knowing how to put an idea across.

I think far too many executives underestimate their ability to work out a terminal period of employment that will simplify and relieve the problems of entering retirement, a tactic that is scarcely mentioned in the literature of retirement.

Of course, such arrangements, being so special and often so at variance with standard procedure, are usually not made known to more people than necessary—another instance of the secrecy surrounding the subject of retirement—and perhaps the people who successfully employ such strategies consider them to be so unique as not to offer any guidance to anyone else. But in my opinion the general principle holds: With a plan in mind and enough years to work it out, most employees with any kind of influence can generally modify and adapt the normal course of events to coincide with their own requirements.

The key, of course, is starting early enough. But there's another vital consideration: Before retirement enters the picture, the long-service employee is at the peak of his power and influence, and his negotiating position is therefore as strong as it will ever be. As retirement grows imminent, negotiating from strength becomes increasingly difficult. But a valued employee in a strategic position would be foolish if he were not to use his leverage with management in his own behalf for objectives other than those for which he has used it all along: for more pay and more power. This time, if he has become aware of his new objective, he will use it to arrange a transition period well in advance of his retirement date.

The idea of "negotiating" retirement seems odd; we are all led to believe that pension plans are inflexible—a misleading notion I will later discuss—and, by inference, so is retirement. The only factor that seems to be variable is the retirement date, in the sense that retirement is usually possible under certain circumstances earlier than the company's policy requires.

The employee is generally informed what benefits he may expect to receive and what options are open to him. These options will almost always concern either the retirement date or the form in which pension payments will be made. It all seems fixed, cut and dried, with scarcely a suggestion that there is any elbow room for adjustment. So far as the actual pension plan is concerned, there generally isn't, and this misleads some otherwise alert executives into overlooking the possibilities of making individual adjustments outside of the plan itself, in the area of general management, where operating executives are constantly making new decisions.

As I have already suggested, the principal areas of adjustment are in terms of the kind of work the employee will be doing in his final working years, the positions he will hold, the scope of his responsibilities, the place where he will be based, and the timing of his retirement, all of these offering possibilities by which the suddenness and totality of retirement can be averted and a transition period of considerable duration can be worked out.

The negotiations to which I refer need not be formally approached—although that is often a good idea, particularly when the employee is in a strategically important post—but can be the result of a slow process of quiet suggestion, of sounding out, of tentative proposals, of carefully maneuvering the idea into the mainstream of management thinking about the future. Sometimes it is possible for agreement to be reached by a consensus arrived at without any negotiation at all, because of the practical force of an idea to which there is no organized opposition. Here is where executives feel most at home; it is the kind of politicking most successful people are good at—which explains why they are successful. They fail to help themselves in this way, I suppose, because they are accustomed to thinking of ways to increase their power rather than taper it off and to increase their incomes rather than begin leveling off or cutting down. Simply because he has this mind-set, the typical executive will scheme very cleverly how to get his income adjusted in his final years so as to maximize his retirement benefits even though they may already be ample. Yet he will not position himself properly for the act of retirement until the very last moment, when it is far too late to make any change in his status.

I am somewhat surprised at the small number of people I have encountered who took advantage of the flexibility of timing that is so frequently possible in planning retirement. Most people start with their "official" retirement date and work backward in their planning, trying to arrange all their affairs to culminate on the target date, and often never seriously considering the possibility of shifting the target to a more advantageous date. Mandatory and official retirement dates are made to seem so immovable as to make any thought of change fruitless. Yet, on closer examination, one sees that in most plans a change of retirement date is not impossible; it almost always requires paying some sort of financial penalty, but sometimes it will make better sense to take the penalty rather than remain pinned to an arbitrary date. And sometimes the penalty is not great.

A potential retiree who has been quietly planning for several years to develop a special assignment for himself that will bridge the jump into retirement may be able to work his plan better, as the time draws near, if he schedules his retirement to coincide with ongoing events rather than try to force events to conform to his retirement schedule.

When the legal mandatory retirement age was postponed

from age sixty-five to age seventy, many people automatically assumed their seventieth birthday as their new target retirement date. Others were aware that they had the option of retiring at age sixty-five or choosing to remain to age seventy. Although it seems fairly obvious once it is put into words, fewer people realized that a great range of other possibilities had been opened: One could retire at sixty-six, sixty-seven, sixty-eight, sixty-nine, or any other point between sixty-five and seventy. To overlook considering all of these possibilities is to shortchange oneself.

It may seem that I am assuming far too much power and influence on the part of the retiree; many people feel they cannot influence the management or the policies of the companies for which they work. Yet almost every employee who has been with a reputable company long enough to qualify for a full-scale pension usually has a good relationship with at least one influential person interested in his welfare. This person might be his direct superior, but often it is a former boss who has moved up and away, or a high executive who has developed a special respect for his abilities. So if the employee cannot act in his own behalf, he can often enlist the aid of his sponsor—for no reason other than goodwill and for no return other than heartfelt appreciation or a way of repaying past loyalties.

A packaging executive three years away from retirement had been developing early warning symptoms of heart disease that his doctors told him would ultimately become worse if he continued too long in his stressful job. He felt he could not afford the financial penalties of taking early retirement; yet he could not continue at his current pace. The company had a practice of continuing to keep on the payroll executives who became gravely ill, sometimes for as long as a year or more. Having arranged a special appointment, he made a proposal to a major company executive, for whom he had worked years before, and who had a high regard for his abilities.

The proposal was that instead of his continuing to work and eventually incurring a mild or severe heart attack, in which case he would be continued at full pay although he might be unproductive for a year or more, the company should spread a year's pay over a two-year period, in effect halving his salary. During that period, he would not work at all—as though he had actually been stricken. Thus, he would have two stress-free years before retirement in which to try to improve his health before it deteriorated further.

Prior to this two-year period before retirement, he would spend a year finding and training a successor and making certain that the work would continue at its high level, without the disruption that would ensue if he had been stricken with a heart attack.

He would take the penalty of two years on half pay, but this reduction would not affect his final retirement pension, and by officially retiring at sixty-five his Social Security payment would be the maximum. The company would be assured of an orderly transition of responsibility from himself to his successor. The employee would, it was hoped, be able to avert the impending health calamity. And the cost to the company was no more than it would have been if he had indeed fallen ill.

It was an idea the company would never have conceived or proposed. By working out a strategy for solving his problem, the employee was able to make a carefully worked-out proposal to his executive friend, who informally discussed it with other company executives, and after a few months it was quietly approved.

I cite this example because it is both unique and complicated, and it illustrates the fact that strategic planning can succeed if the strategy is sound, that exceptions can be and are made, that there are special solutions for special cases, and that people can edge their way into retirement by many different pathways, if they have a clear idea of where and how they want to go.

In this case, the employee was concerned about protecting his health from further deterioration, but he gained one thing more that he had not really thought about: During the year in which he was training his successor, he gradually released his responsibilities to him and thus had an interval in which to taste the flavor of retirement before it became a finality. Even the reduction in pay had its beneficial side effects: It was a way of rehearsing how to live on his retirement pay. And this was followed by two years of what the company regarded as sick leave but which he recognized as a form of early retirement, although he was still officially employed. This helped considerably in making a slower transition.

Finally, it illustrates that although *pension* plans are not considered flexible, *retirement* plans can be, and there are all sorts of modifications that can be made outside the terms of the pension plan itself. I have concluded that no matter how ingenious people may be at making arrangements to enhance their retirement income, they have not done as much or as well for themselves as they could have if they had also worked out the optimum strategy for approaching and entering retirement. It might be stated as a dictum that the man who has made no attempt to negotiate the circumstances of his own retirement may have cheated himself.

Retirement planning is so overwhelmingly focused on financial matters that it is quite possible to lose sight of the fact that there are other considerations perhaps as important or more so. And it is so overwhelmingly focused on maximizing financial resources that another essential idea is often obscured: the little-discussed possibility that it is sometimes wiser to *reduce* income or to *spend* capital in order to make for a better retirement.

The packaging executive I have described gave up a year's pay over the two-year final period. He regained some of it with two years additional Social Security credit and lost less of it by dropping into a lower tax bracket, but his attitude was that if he had died of a heart attack he would have lost everything.

Here's what seems to me a sensible point of view: If we recognize the wisdom and necessity of investing in our careers when we are young, devoting years of our lives and huge sums to educate and prepare ourselves, we should also be able to recognize the wisdom and often the necessity of investing both time and money in preparing ourselves for retirement. Yet we tend to feel impoverished if we do anything that lessens our income or our capital, and wasteful if we spend any substantial amount of time in getting ready to retire.

I know a couple who sold their home in Chicago and bought one in Asheville; after a year they knew they had made a mistake and bitterly regretted being unable to go back to their Chicago home, where they had been so comfortable.

"Instead of selling one home and buying another, why didn't you just keep the Chicago house for a year or so, and live in Asheville until you knew which place was best for you?"

They seemed surprised the answer wasn't already obvious to me. "We couldn't afford to maintain two homes," she said.

A little arithmetic disclosed that it would have been a very expensive year, indeed—almost twice their normal overhead. In terms of "living within their means"—which means their current income—it would seem foolishly extravagant. But when I asked them to think of it as a capital investment,

the extra cost came to less than 3 percent of their capital.
"Would you be willing to pay three percent of your
savings to go back to your original home in Chicago?" I
asked. And of course they would.

These are little tricks of perception and misperception.
The same expenditure seems extravagant considered as an
expense but sensible considered as an investment. Our generation seems insufficiently conditioned to be able to think
of investing in anything intangible or unprofitable at retirement; it is difficult for them to think of investing in keeping
their options open, in experiments that might not work, in
activities and life-styles that might not prove suitable, although it may well be argued that to do so is prudent, not
foolish.

In my view it is far better to work out a satisfying retirement life on a smaller budget than to endure a dismal retirement that is well financed.

Of all the profound points of view that can be expressed
about retirement, one of the most meaningful, to me, is that
retirement requires investment; for what we really invest in
it are our years, however many or few remain to us. This is
capital, indeed, and, unlike our financial resources, cannot
be replenished or replaced.

The tragedy of the couple from Chicago, I felt, was that
they had lost the better part of a year by spending it unhappily in Asheville, and they would continue spending time
unhappily until they worked out some other solution. This
seemed to me a poor trade-off to avoid spending money at a
higher rate for a limited time.

Once we think in terms of spending and investing years—
of a limited number allotted to us—rather than solely of
spending dollars, there are substantial changes in our value
system, and these, in turn, may influence our strategy for
retirement.

We are so conditioned to believe that our purpose in life is to achieve our career goals that it is difficult to see it from any other point of view. But consider how much would change in the way the world looks to us if we take a different angle of vision, just out of curiosity, and think of our working life as our investment in attaining a satisfactory retirement. From this point of view, each year a person continues working represents an investment of a year of his life. The proper strategy for some, then, might be to find ways to get the most retirement for the least investment, which is another way of saying, to retire as early as possible.

Applied to a more familiar problem, it goes like this: A person has a pension plan that enables him to retire at age sixty-five on a pension of $1,000 a month. If he retires at sixty-four, his pension is reduced 10 percent. What he is considering, then, is to spend a year of his life to increase his pension by $100 a month. The question is: Should he invest a year of his life for an annual added income of $1,200?

Each person must answer such questions for himself, although few will express it in such terms; too many simply take it for granted that the best strategy is to get the highest possible pension, whatever it is. But consider this: Suppose this person will live only until he is seventy. He does not know this, of course, but he does know that he is mortal and will not live forever. To have spent one year of the six years he will live, in order to increase his annual income by $1,200 for the remaining five years means spending one-sixth of his remaining lifetime to get $6,000. Only he can make this choice between time and money; it is not my purpose to advocate any particular decision, but rather to point out that this view of investment illuminates the entire matter of scheduling retirement and of managing the money for it.

XXIV. SHAPING MORE
FAVORABLE CIRCUMSTANCES

*If you start early enough and know what you want,
you might influence events to work in your favor.*

I HAVE MENTIONED the reluctance of operating executives
to think about or plan for retirement, as well as their reluctance to have their associates think of them as soon to
be retired. For this reason most exhortations to plan early
go unheeded, particularly by those who view retirement as
a personal calamity, one which has a kind of inevitability
about it. It seems subject to very little control, like an act of
nature. "You cannot stop the storm; you can only try to
build the best shelter."

This feeling of being helpless to alter the inevitable is
partially a myth deriving from some of the mystery of retirement as well as the mystery of pension plans. I have tried
to show that there is generally a good potential for adjusting
the circumstances surrounding retirement, so as to make
them more favorable in ways other than financial. The greatest asset any executive has in this respect is the almost unlimited length of time in which he can devise and work toward
the set of circumstances he has in mind. He can alter his
retirement date to fit them, or try to fit them to his date.
He can make all sorts of individual and private arrangements

and reach private understandings about his ending years—what work he will do, where he will do it, and what changes, up or down, may be made in his compensation. Looked at this way, the incentive to think and plan may well overcome the inertia of trying to ignore the inevitable.

There is still another kind of power the executive can employ in his own behalf, giving an additional incentive for careful advance planning: He sometimes forgets that companies are constantly reviewing and adjusting their employee benefits and that, given enough time and a clear objective, it may be possible to influence the kinds of benefits that will be available to him when his retirement date arrives. What muddies thinking along these lines is generally the fact that "retirement benefits" are considered loosely as referring to the pension plan. And that, as all executives know, is a tangle of such incomprehensibility that it is almost always interpreted to employees in one-syllable language and in broad generalities, with a footnote disclaiming any conflict between these oversimplifications and the plan itself.

But, surrounding the plan itself, there is always a set of company practices; some are formally expressed as plans, while others may be informal courtesies or customs of the company. It would be wise for any executive, beginning to think of his retirement still some years ahead, to take a close look at these benefits. First, because he should know what his entitlements are: those that will come to him automatically, those that are available only if requested, and those that are discretionary at the whim of management. Second, because there may be ways, given enough time, to bring about improvements that accord with his needs. Companies will rarely offer new benefits in which their employees express no interest; they will generally consider—perhaps not enact, but consider—those in which their employees seem to have a good deal of interest.

"My company had a tuition-refund plan whereby within a certain time of retirement employees could take courses to learn new skills and develop interests and hobbies. There was nothing in this idea that interested me, and I never took advantage of it. But Mary had returned to school to get her Master's because she knew it would open up all sorts of possibilities for her after we had retired. A few months before I retired, we were going over her tuition costs, and she asked me why my company didn't include her in their tuition plan. I had never thought about that, and the next day I asked the Personnel Office whether the plan extended to wives.

"The Personnel Manager said the plan only covered company employees. 'This is the first time anyone has ever asked for tuition for a spouse,' he told me. 'Actually, it's not a bad idea; I'll mention it at the next meeting.' And about a year after I retired, they did add spouses to the plan—too late to do me any good."

An employee with a clear understanding of how he and his family will proceed along the road to his retirement might improve his prospects as he goes along; in this case, had he been thinking in terms of retirement benefits, he almost certainly could have brought about an improvement in the tuition-refund plan that would have benefited him. It may have required bringing up the idea to a few other employees and having them make similar inquiries at the Personnel Office, simply to signal that this was a subject employees were interested in. But even if that were not so, he might have arranged for someone to authorize an exception in his case whereby his wife's tuition would be completely or partially paid.

The essential idea is the awareness that *one can influence events*, that there is more flexibility than one may assume, and that the vital element is sufficient advance knowledge of what you want the company to do to make your retirement easier.

In a company that, from time to time, gave stock options to certain classes of executives, there was one employee two years away from retirement who received such an option and realized that, as he could exercise only 20 percent of the option each year over the next five years, he would be able to exercise only 40 percent before he would retire and the option would be automatically canceled. Sixty percent of its value would be lost.

"It's just too late to do anything about that now," the company treasurer told him. "If you had brought it up more than five years before your retirement, we could have—and probably would have—taken into account that we were giving you your last full allotment before retirement. But nobody thought of it in time—*not even you.*"

Another executive was troubled by the uncertainties of the company's annual salary review. His retirement pension would be based on the highest three of the last five earnings years. However, there was no way of knowing what his earnings would be in his final five years, as the annual salary reviews gave unpredictable results. A change in management might result in his work being appraised by a new supervisor; all sorts of unexpected factors could affect the five separate annual judgments that would be made.

He made an ingenious proposal to his management: that the practice of making annual appraisals for purposes of salary review should stop five years prior to an employee's retirement; at that time a single five-year review should be made and a salary progression schedule set up establishing the dates and amounts of all salary adjustments in the final five years. These would be routinely activated unless the quality of the employee's work fell significantly below his already established level of performance.

This would enable him to plan his financial situation with fairly firm figures and to get a reliable calculation of the amount of his pension. He pointed out that it was highly questionable whether annual performance appraisals and routine merit reviews continue to be appropriate in the final stages of a long career, and that it was important to know his pension base in advance.

He was not able to lobby this change into effect before his own final five-year period began, but he was able to achieve his purposes anyway. He proposed that management try out the idea in a few selected instances to see how it worked out. He thereby became the "test case" that led to a change of company policy long after he had retired.

I mention such examples to illustrate a little-recognized and underutilized asset that many preretirees possess: the capacity to effect change.

It is by thinking along these lines that the act of retirement becomes less an event imposed upon the employee by some impersonal fate and more a set of circumstances designed and created by the individual to best serve his own purposes.

XXV. AVOIDING PENSION PITFALLS

Some quick-and-dirty arithmetic demonstrating that the pension you expect is not always what you get—and how to protect yourself.

I MENTIONED THAT pension plans are generally considered fixed and inflexible, but they prove to be greatly variable once their mystery is stripped away. They are mysterious because they are incomprehensible to a layman and almost always require an interpreter to tell us what the language means. Thus, almost all the information any employee ever acquires about his pension status or entitlement is a tale told at second hand, someone's interpretation of the way the pension plan applies to him. It rests fundamentally on faith: our willingness to accept what we are told because we cannot think of a good reason anyone would want to deceive or defraud us, and because whatever the company tells us seems to square with what we have already been told.

For this reason, although some people do ask what their pension status and rights are (and others simply wait to be informed), few know what specific questions to ask. It seems to me to be vital for anyone in a pension plan to keep well informed of his status and, especially when he comes to within five years of retirement, to check and recheck everything. To wait until formal retirement is far too late to find or correct possible errors and mistaken assumptions.

I will give you a highly simplified example, bypassing a tangle of technicalities, modifications, exceptions, and variations that would confuse rather than enlighten: You are told early in your employment that the company's pension plan is designed to enable people to retire on 50 percent of their "final average salary." The "final average salary" is defined in your plan as the average of the three highest earning years of the five complete calendar years preceding retirement. You are normally due to retire when you are sixty-five.

This formula sounds so simple, there does not seem to be anything to question; you feel you could estimate your probable pension figure in a few moments. At retirement, however, you may discover that the actual pension you are paid is quite different from the one you expected. Why?

Let's look first at the "five complete calendar years preceding retirement." If you retire in 1983, you would expect the five complete preceding years to be 1982–81–80–79–78, right? Not necessarily, because we must first establish the technically correct retirement date. You might expect that date to be, say, March 21, 1983, the date of your sixty-fifth birthday. But that may not be correct, because, depending on the plan and the way it is administered, you may always be the age of your nearest birthday. If so, you became sixty-five a half year earlier than your sixty-fifth birthday, on September 22, 1982, because on that date you were closer to your sixty-fifth birthday than to your sixty-fourth, and the company may consider that to be your normal retirement date for actuarial purposes. In such event, the "five complete calendar years preceding retirement" are moved back a year, becoming the years 1981–80–79–78–77, and the higher salaries for 1982 and 1983 are not included in the calculations and do not improve your pension payout.

So, if you made $30,000 a year in 1981, $28,000 in 1980, and $26,000 in 1979 (and less in 1978 and 1977), your final average salary will be the average of these three highest years, or $28,000, despite the fact that on the day of your retirement you may be earning at the annual rate of $34,000.

But there are a few more hidden considerations. What was your salary in 1981? Did I just say it was $30,000? Sorry. I was thinking of the salary you were making at the *end* of the year. Remember, you *began* the year at $28,000 and got the $2,000 raise during March when your annual salary review is made. I don't know (and you won't unless you ask) what the plan considers your 1981 salary to be—the annual rate you were being paid at the end of the year ($30,000) or the annual rate you were being paid at the beginning of the year ($28,000) or the actual total salary you received over the twelve calendar months ($29,500). The chances are it will be one of the two lower amounts. When we correct all three years, and find the average of $29,500, $27,500, and $25,500, we establish a pension base of $27,500.

All right, then, you can expect a pension of 50 percent of that base, or $13,750, right? Well, not exactly. You have been receiving a $1,000 bonus every year, which you always considered to be part of your salary. But under the plan, the final average salary excludes bonuses, overtime pay, and other perks; it deals solely with straight pay. So we'll take out the bonuses, reduce the base to $26,500, and take 50 percent of that, right? We're now down to a pension of $13,250, okay? Well. . . .

What you haven't taken into account is that this pension plan, like most plans, is "integrated." That means that your company, which has been paying half of your Social Security contribution all these years, figures that half the Social Security payment you will get is really part of their pension plan payment. If your Social Security payment is $6,600, $3,300 of that is deducted from the $13,250 you expected the company to pay you, so you will get only $9,950 from them. Is that the bottom line, then? Well, almost, but not exactly.

We've been making certain assumptions of which you may not be aware. One assumption is that you have served the full thirty years required by your plan to retire on a full pension. If you served only twenty-five years, that $13,250 would be reduced by a sixth, to $11,041, and deducting the $3,300 Social Security would take it down to $7,741. But let's take the more cheerful assumption that you have worked the full thirty years, so we can go back to the $9,950 you expect to get.

But that figure is based on still another assumption: It was assumed that you would select a certain way of taking your pension. In this example, your company assumes, for purposes of illustration, that everyone will take the normal mode called "Ten Years Certain and Continuous." This means that you or your heirs will get the pension for ten years; after that, it will continue if you live but stop as soon as you die.

But what about my wife? you may ask. What happens to her when I die and my pension stops? Not to worry, you will be told, the plan offers various options. You can arrange for your pension to continue through your widow's lifetime, and for her to get 100 percent of your pension, 75 percent, 50 percent, or whatever percentage you choose.

The catch is that all these alternatives will further reduce your pension. For example, if you want your wife to receive 75 percent of your pension after you die, your pension when you retire will not be $9,950, but $8,753, and your widow would get $6,565 after you die for as long as she lives.

Let's drop this example—it has already served my purpose, which was not to teach you about pension plans but to show you that although you may be earning at the rate of $34,000 when you retire, the "50 percent pension" you expect might be 25 percent to start with and shrink to 19 percent after you've gone.

You have not done justice to yourself or your family if you wait until impending retirement to make such discoveries. But I have something more in mind: It is to caution you that company records are not as infallible as you would like them to be. You may have found errors in your paycheck from time to time and may have had them corrected, but you have no way of knowing whether the corrections were ever picked up in your pension records. You have no way of knowing whether your pension file shows the right employment date for you—it is based on records that go back, probably, a quarter century or more to when you were first hired. And you don't know whether the leave of absence you took fifteen years ago is now being interpreted as having broken the continuity of your employment. So you don't know that you have been credited properly with your years of service. You cannot assume that the pension file has picked up the right salary data, both as to amounts and effective dates, or even that it gives your birthdate or your wife's age correctly. The fact is, you don't even know that the arithmetic of your pension calculations is correct.

To attempt to check these things out when you approach retirement is foolhardy and often simply not possible. And, if errors are disclosed, the task of correcting them is formidable. I know of only one sensible course of action: to start checking early and to assume nothing until you have evidence for it. It is true that there is probably no one who has any reason to try to defraud you and it may also be true that each annual pension statement you receive seems to pick up where the prior one left off—but the statements may be perpetuating errors that date back to earlier days, to other systems and different records, kept by long-gone employees.

So, preferably more than five years away from retirement, you should begin checking what the records actually say about you—not the records in the handy personnel reference files, but specifically the formal pension records, which may be in an entirely different department. And you should begin the process of checking the entire range of options your pension plan actually offers you, finding out what methods the company plan uses to establish your final average salary, your length of service, your salary history, your actuarial age, your normal retirement date, verifying that you have been fully credited and that the company records are accurate in every particular, challenging any that diminish your pension, and, finally, finding out as early as possible how much money you will actually receive every month in dollars and cents, from the time you retire until you die, and what happens to your pension after that.

XXVI. SOME CHARACTERISTICS
OF SUCCESS

Activity, diversity, and connection with others are among the hallmarks of successful retirement.

THE VARIETY OF human experience is infinite, even in retirement. For many people, perhaps for most, a pattern for living eventually emerges that serves their purpose. We must remember not to expect more of life, or of ourselves, after we retire than before. Retired or not, some people enjoy their lives fully, others do not, and most of us fall between the two. The experience of retirement changes us, but it does not transform us into other people; we remain who we were, and our skills and innate capacities in the art of living continue to define the way we respond to our life experiences.

Once people have learned, however painfully, how to become retired persons and have managed to traverse the whitewater rapids we all pass through on that voyage, they generally do come to more navigable waters, a stream that flows more quietly and smoothly, and they make of it whatever they can and respond to it in their own way.

I have met many people who are content in retirement (they tend to prefer words such as contentment and satisfaction rather than happiness and joy), and although each has worked out a separate and different pattern, there is a common thread, a somewhat universal quality, that has several components.

One is calmness: They have found ways to turn down the thermostat, to reduce the heat and the fever. "I'm much less impatient—and I don't get all worked up over things I can't do anything about."

This calmness is attributed by some to a feeling of security, a feeling that "things have finally come together and fallen into place." The crucial life problems have been resolved, the major life adjustments—school, career, marriage, parenthood, retirement—have been made. Others have told me their calmness is the result of their no longer having to live at their outer limits, that they have been able to fall back enough to develop a store of inner reserves and resources they can call on. In others it has been described as "no longer chasing my tail," which I translate to mean not wasting enormous amounts of energy reaching for illusory goals, foolish dreams, childish fantasies, and all the mythical kinds of happiness we grew up believing in, and which repeatedly led us to disillusionment. We now can recognize what is and is not possible for us.

One man said, "I know now that having made it this far, which is farther than I ever could imagine, and having gone through and survived everything that has happened to me along the way, I'm going to be able to go the rest of the way from here on. The future no longer seems so mysterious, and it no longer can frighten me. I've had my experience of dealing with it—my future came and I did deal with it, and it has given me confidence in my ability to cope."

The "successfully" retired people invariably are active. Activity is relative, of course, and what may seem like a great deal to one person is little for another. But *in their own terms* every well-adjusted retired person has maintained (or taken on) some level of obligation to *something other than himself*.

214

This takes remarkably diverse forms—all kinds of volunteer work and social service, some through organizations and others as private as maintaining a vegetable garden to aid a needy neighbor.

The distinction as I see it is not in the level of busy-ness; it is not how much time was spent, or energy, or how much is accomplished or what comes of it all: The operative factor is *connection*—the maintenance of linkage between the self and other selves. It is almost as though this were a life support, like a diver's air hose, through which energy is expended and replenished and life is sustained.

I know a retired college professor who had lost her vision and who asked for student volunteers to read to her. I was under the impression that this was her way of continuing her favorite avocation—reading. But in a quiet moment she told me that her real purpose was to continue her contact with the students and to hear what some of these young people thought about the ideas in the books she asked them to read to her. The students, who vied for the privilege of reading to her, considered her to be a most unusual person, so vital and alive and (something to ponder on) so different from people her age.

The other universal component is diversity. The well-adjusted found ways to get a mix into their relationships and avoided ghettoizing themselves in their peer group. They are people who in one way or another have contact with other generations and with people who are not social counterparts of themselves, who are in some ways different in education, background, economic status, ethnicity, or religion.

And finally, when the crisis of retirement is weathered, and the marriage has withstood the buffeting, there is the final peace that is neither truce nor surrender. Both partners know the stormy years are finally over and will never come again, and the ground on which they now stand will not shift. Each has reached a self-sufficiency that permits a giving of strength to the other without feeling threatened by the other's dependency.

Thinking over this brief list of conditions so hard to attain, I cannot help but feel that those who like myself have struggled through to this state in life have gained something of value that we may not have sought and probably could not have found by any other path.

XXVII. CHANGING OUR
PERSONAL VALUES

To go anywhere, we must leave where we are; to become anything else, we must stop being what we were.

THE THINGS OF VALUE in this life are not easily won or even readily recognized. One of the things that gives retirement value but also makes it difficult is that it requires us to change not only the way we spend our time but our value system, too.

Change is always hard, but part of the special difficulty in changing the values we live by is that we rarely have examined them very closely. As a matter of course, many of us, particularly the middle class, value power, acquisition, progress, and security: power over others and the power to control our own lives, our environment, and our possessions; the acquisition of such material comforts and conveniences as an enviable car, a nice home, a good wardrobe, a well-equipped kitchen; progress in such forms as upward mobility, promotion, a better job title, more income, a better college for the kids, a more luxurious vacation, a more prestigious car, more impressive friends; and of course the security of social and professional recognition and steadily growing financial reserves.

Put aside the endless discussion one could have about such values. The point I want to make is that in retirement we must change them. In retirement, security does not increase, the upper limits of upward mobility have already been reached. Power, if it does not shrink, does not grow. The time for acquiring turns into a time for disposing of things no longer needed. The second car and the vacation may be unnecessary. The kids are out on their own. In retirement, we no longer strive for promotions, raises, and better titles, and we no longer have access to the power our titles conferred. We will not get much richer or better known than we already are, or stronger or healthier, for that matter. We don't really need the big house and all those things in it. We have no more college bills to pay. We're as secure as we'll ever be, and the nest egg is ready to hatch. Old friends are passing away or moving away. We are no longer in charge of anything except ourselves.

At retirement, we feel we have finished with all the important things and what remains seems comparatively trivial, not enough to devote our lives to. Our list has outlived its usefulness, and we need a new one, another value system with enough substance to build a new life upon. It must represent more than a set of platitudes such as "enjoy yourself" or "stay young." To do this is not easy, for the only place inside ourselves we can look for new values is among those that weren't very high on our first list. And that means making fundamental changes in our reasons for living.

It took many years, not just in time but in life experience, for each of us to develop our original value system. It does not seem realistic to expect that we can create a new one overnight.

For this reason it is important to start trying to bring our values into focus several years before. Not that this problem can be solved in advance with a ready-made answer; there is no way to enter retirement prepared with a switch button to activate a new set of values. But the better you understand the task awaiting you, the readier you may be to tackle it when you come to it. For that, you would need to know yourself rather well—and since you're going to spend all your retirement in your own company, the effort of getting to know more about the purpose and meaning of your life will surely be worthwhile.

I have tried to offer hard and practical reasons why early thinking about retirement is rewarding; all of these rewards, you may have noted, fall within the value system of the practical executive. But there is little chance of gratification in retirement if we do not begin to question the value system itself. Does it continue to be effective and appropriate outside the context of the business world? I have described the conflict between the conditioned responses we have acquired in our careers and the realities of the lives of retired people— even the clash between the business culture and the world of home and family.

Part of the act of retiring, I have come to believe, is the act of altering, perhaps reversing, the values we have been living by, a slow and difficult process that must begin long before we put our value system to the test of retirement.

This may be an aspect more suitable for philosophers, priests, or psychologists, but it cannot be left unremarked; I promised to suggest some points of view, angles of vision, and ways of thinking that might make a difference not simply in what we plan and do but in how we see such things and our attitudes toward them.

A handy way to think of retirement is to picture it as a space capsule atop a first-stage booster rocket. The first stage is an unwieldy, monstrous, powerful thing whose only purposes are to go higher and faster; it is by far the larger of the two. The second-stage capsule is comparatively tiny, and for a long time it seems to have no function at all, sitting there idle and dormant atop the first stage.

The first stage, which can be an analogy for our working lives, provides the long journey during which we expend all our energies on driving forward and upward. Like our careers, its purpose is to get us as high as possible as fast as possible. Finally and inevitably, when we have reached the farthermost place from our starting point, when our elevation is highest and our speed the greatest, its function is completed and its capacities exhausted. It is useless and now becomes a cumbersome impediment and a mass of dead weight. If all has been well arranged, this is the time it is released and left to fall away.

Now for the first time the second stage, the retirement capsule, comes alive. It is comparatively small, but it is agile. It can change direction, turn on its own axis, move into any attitude, all the while traveling faster than the first stage ever could. It can change orbits on very small impulses. It can perform actions that were impossible before. It is free of almost all restraints. It can go into space rarely or never visited, provide views never before seen, link itself to others, land on strange moons.

This analogy provides the flavor I want to convey of the possibilities of retirement. If retirement is viewed as the culmination of our career drives, if it can be seen as dropping the first stage of the rocket, we can see that there is little to regret in the completion of the first stage of our lives—it has served its purpose and it has launched us into a place we could never have reached without it.

Now, in our so-much-smaller retirement capsule, for which we need so much less fuel, we have gained control and power and freedom to a far greater extent than we have ever had them. What we do with these things depends on what we want. Increased speed and increased height are no longer sensible goals; we need other purposes now. These purposes are rooted in whatever value system we hold at the time we arrive at this stage of our lives—but clearly they should be different from the ones we held during our rocketing upward journey.

I have said that the things we are concerned about are the things that give us our identity: We are what we care about. So, long before retirement, it is important to begin to examine what concerns we will have when the first stage burns out, when we no longer need to win, no longer need to compete, no longer need to increase our earning power, no longer need to dominate anyone else. What do we need then?

It has been said in many ways that what everyone needs is someone to care about, and someone who cares about him (or her). In our working lives we do not often get a chance to express *caring* in this sense, and we do not often make contact with other human beings on a human level. We grow out of the habit, deprecate what we call "weakness" or "softness" and learn to couch even our arguments for the humane treatment of others in terms of hard, real, or practical advantages because we sense that saying "It would be a kind thing to do" is never considered a sufficient reason for doing anything in the business world.

The operating executive, then, before he retires, must look outside the business world for an opportunity to make human linkages, to develop or regain his ability to *care*, to learn to be comfortable in a permissive environment, not to feel embarrassed to have emotional responses. What does this mean? It means different things for different people, but fundamentally it means turning more consciously to the family and the home, or to a larger community, for things and people to care about; it means making commitments to others, to causes and purposes; it means learning how to tolerate *involvement* in the lives of other people. It means thinking in terms of giving and sharing. It means, in a sense, participating in the human search for *community*, a far more widespread quest than many people realize.

These things take time and energy, which working people consider so valuable they do all they can to conserve them. But the psychic rewards and satisfactions people seem to find in humane endeavors seem to be energizing and, to the extent that they may impinge on the time one's career demands, they may impose small penalties which may be well worth paying.

What I am saying here is that there must be developed a focus in one's life other than the focus—the all-consuming intensity—of successfully earning a living. Lacking it, when the process of earning a living ends, there will be no focus at all. So it is not a bad thing to learn fairly early that business success is not and cannot be all and that one can wean oneself away from it as a preparation for ending it altogether.

Here two major streams begin to flow together, for we have also to consider the effect of a man's retirement on his wife and family. Many of the negative effects I have mentioned are rooted in his business-oriented responses and his detachment from the dynamics of daily family life long before retirement. If he has begun to consider its possible effect on his wife, he should be aware that there are changes ahead for her as well as for him.

There is no better way to begin to learn how to enact caring and sharing than for each partner to become concerned with the ways in which the future may affect the other, and to plan these changes so that they complement and supplement each other.

There is no better way to open—or reopen—human communication than on the basis of concern for the other and for the other's needs. "Let's explore what possibilities would open up for you if I were retired," a man may say to his wife and learn something of her own vision of the future for herself.

222

Or, if she has no such vision, he may help her to find one. Certainly, he can help her to think of ways to make possible what she may have assumed to be beyond reach, or unreasonable. There are adjustments and modifications each can make in his or her plans, timetables, and objectives to accommodate to the other, once they have begun to talk openly to each other about it. For it is just as important for her to have a plan as it is for him, especially if she is a career woman or has a career in mind.

The commitment each is making to the other, probably without ever saying so, is that each will help the other grow as a separate person, and the extent of their caring will be the link that binds them together.

This process must lead to a change of values, as it is intended to. More, it makes retirement a time that can be anticipated rather than dreaded, puts it into a more meaningful shape and strips it of its threatening vagueness.

What it comes down to is a reaching out—beyond the business world—for human and personal values that do not exist in that world, and development of the ability to discard the values of that world when it comes time to leave it.

This cannot be adopted simply as a course of action, as one might go on a weight-reduction diet or take up jogging for health; it is a slow search for new insights, and these do not come in an orderly sequence or as a planned program. They evolve slowly over a period of time, and always in unexpected ways. The idea is simply to try to make oneself susceptible to them, to try to nurture them, and not to be embarrassed by them even if they seem to contradict other values we have been holding. Although I do not want to hold myself up as an example, I can best cite from my own experience one of the ways my own values changed in such a process.

In my preretirement years, my wife and I found it hard

to visualize ourselves as retired people. Without her work and mine, with our children grown, our friends scattered, we felt we would have to find something to put in place of the rootless and purposeless existence that seemed to lie ahead. We also began to consider the plight of either of us if and when the other would pass away, or become handicapped or bedridden, and so began to think of how to bring other people into our lives. There are many ways one can do this; the way that we started to explore was suggested to us by a woman we met at a lecture we attended. She told us about an experiment in communal living, a three-week exercise that summer in learning how people can share their lives with one another, although they begin as strangers.

We surprised ourselves by remaining open to the possibilities of the idea, although it was one we considered exotic, potentially embarrassing, and completely out of key with the sensible and conventional life-style with which we felt comfortable. That summer experience led us to see that there were others—men and women, young and old, from all walks of life—who like us were looking for ways to reach out beyond their own lives to other human beings. We began exploring ways in which we might join forces with other like-thinking people and began to learn something of the commune movement in the United States.

As a result, we spent almost a year after our retirement visiting various kinds of voluntary communities, the diversity of which was beyond belief. We never did find the right place for us, but the experience of exploring the ways people's lives were enhanced by trusting one another, caring for and about one another, sharing with one another, slowly displaced some of our own personal values, and we found ourselves acting, feeling, and relating to other people differently, and in more satisfying ways. We could not have planned for this result; but we did consciously try to let it happen.

Other people go in by other doors: One family we admire took into their home a Vietnamese refugee family, helped them learn English, get medical care, learn American ways, get their children into school, learn to support themselves, find a home of their own, and eventually become self-sufficient. For the host family, this experience accomplished many of the things that our experience with shared living taught us.

After more than twenty-five years of marriage, my wife and I thought we knew each other pretty well, but it was only a long while after we had begun talking about our views of retirement that we discovered we had each misperceived the other's needs. My concern for her had revolved around the question of what she would do without me, how she could survive if I were not at her side. Her concern for me, I learned, was similar: how I could get along without her.

But, as we talked, each of us learned that we each considered ourselves to be the stronger of the two, that neither of us felt weaker or more dependent, and that our real needs were not so much how to give help to the other as much as how to enable each of us to use our own strengths fully for ourselves. As a result, we each began to think more freely about ourselves, without feeling that we were depriving the other of some sort of essential support. In a way, we found we were far stronger than each of us had thought, and this, too, changed our plans, our lives, and our relationship.

These are small examples of the way change can come about if it is deliberately sought, provoked, and courted. So perhaps a word about change is pertinent here. Change is a fundamental law of life, so it seems strange we should be so resistant to it. We try to hold on when we should let go. Perhaps this is because our culture values more highly the person who holds on than the one who lets go. We also see the person who hangs in there with bulldog determination as the active one, the person who lets go and gives in as passive.

Do these perspectives square in any way with our life experience? I think not.

It seems to me that life is a constant process of letting go, not of holding on. Our inability to let go seems to determine in large measure how much of a struggle life will be.

Nothing continues except change; nothing remains the same, nor should it. Life is not a state of being, but a process of becoming. To go anywhere, we must leave where we are, to become anything else, we must stop being what we were. To climb the ladder, we must take our foot off one rung to place it on the next, else we cannot rise. We must let go of childhood before we can become adults, let go of school when we start work, let go of "home" when we marry, and let go of our children when they become responsible for themselves. We let go of our careers when we retire and, looking well into the future, we know that ultimately we will have to let go of vigor, of old friends, of familiar neighborhoods and ways of life, and inevitably of life itself, and if we have mastered the difficult art we can do these things with grace and dignity.

To resist change, to try to hang on and hold on, is a futile attempt to stop the flow of the natural order. It is to be like a tree that will not bend, a swimmer who clings to the edge of the pool, a child who refuses to grow up.

It is not easy to let go, but it is never really possible to hold on. We may mourn the loss of our childhood and innocence but we cannot retain them long. Much of our anguish in life arises from our being unwilling or unable to allow life to proceed, to fully release the brake, to accept change without struggle.

Letting go is a life skill and it requires a kind of learned courage, but in our culture there are opposite values that retard our ability to develop it. We give our applause to the one who doggedly tries to swim upstream rather than to the truly brave adventurer who floats on the surging currents that bear him through unfamiliar places toward some unknown and ever-changing destination.

If we have anticipated and accepted the inevitability of change and have learned the art of letting go, we can turn away from a completed career with no more sense of loss than we might feel for the depleted first stage of a space vehicle. By letting go of it, we set ourselves free for the next stage of our lifelong journey, to explore our inner selves and find our outer limits.